Quality Assurance Interview Q & A

SHUBHAM MISHRA

SHIVANGI DWIVEDI

First edition
Published: 12 December, 2022
ISBN: 978-93-5891-469-6

This book is dedicated to all aspiring quality assurance professionals.
~ Shubham Mishra

This book is dedicated to all my dear readers.
~ Shivangi Dwivedi

Contents

Preface

Welcome to the world of Quality Assurance! Quality assurance plays a critical role in ensuring that software applications meet the required standards of quality, reliability, and usability. The software industry has seen a significant surge in demand for Quality Assurance professionals in recent years. The primary objective of Quality Assurance is to make sure that the software application meets the end user's expectations and requirements.

The Quality Assurance Interview Q & A book is designed to provide an extensive range of interview questions and answers that will help both novice and experienced Quality Assurance professionals prepare for job interviews. The book covers a broad range of topics that QA professionals will encounter during interviews, including quality assurance processes, testing methodologies, test management, test automation, defect tracking, and more.

The book is divided into chapters based on topics, with each chapter containing a list of questions and answers that are frequently asked during interviews. The questions are designed to cover a wide range of experience levels, from entry-level to senior-level QA professionals. Each answer is explained in detail, with practical examples, tips, and best practices that will help you understand the topic better.

The book is a valuable resource for job seekers who are looking to land their dream job in QA. It can also be used as a reference guide for experienced QA professionals who want to enhance their knowledge and keep up-to-date with the latest trends and best practices in the industry.

We hope you find this book useful in your journey toward becoming a successful Quality Assurance professional. Happy reading and best of luck with your interviews!

Acknowledgement

I would like to express my heartfelt gratitude to the many individuals who have contributed to the creation of this Quality Assurance Q & A book.

Firstly, I am deeply grateful to **My Parents, Mr. A.K. Mishra and Mrs. Mamta Mishra**, for their unwavering belief in my abilities. Without their constant support and encouragement, writing this book would not have been possible.

I extend my heartfelt thanks to my **Co-author Shivangi Dwivedi** for her invaluable contribution to this book.

I express my heartfelt gratitude to **Team Pothi (https://www.pothi.com)** for their priceless assistance and direction in publishing the first edition of this book.

I would like to express my gratitude to the Almighty for providing me with the strength, guidance, and inspiration to write this book. Without His blessings, this endeavor would not have been possible.

Finally, I would like to express my gratitude to all the readers of this book, as it would not have been possible without your interest and support. I hope this book serves as a helpful resource in preparing for quality assurance interviews and advancing your career in this field.

Shubham Mishra

Acknowledgement

I would like to express my deepest gratitude to **My Parents, Mr. Girish Dwivedi and Mrs. Rashmi Dwivedi**, for their unconditional love and support throughout this journey of writing the Quality Assurance Interview Q & A book.

I would like to express my gratitude to my **Co-author Shubham Mishra**, whose collaboration and support were invaluable in bringing this book to fruition. His expertise and insights were instrumental in shaping the content of this book.

I extend my heartfelt thanks to **Team Pothi** (https://www.pothi.com), who believed in my work and provided me with the opportunity to share my knowledge with a broader audience.

I cannot forget to acknowledge the readers of this book, who are the ultimate beneficiaries of my efforts. I hope this book has been a valuable resource for them.

Lastly, I would like to thank God for giving me the strength and inspiration to complete this book.

Shivangi Dwivedi

About Shubham Mishra

Shubham Mishra is India's youngest cybersecurity expert and a leading name in the field of ethical hacking. He is the founder and CEO of TOAE Security Solutions and has dedicated his life to the robust development of cybersecurity methods that are being used worldwide. Shubham has worked with some of the largest companies in the world for more than a decade and continues to provide updated and relevant content for the industry.

You can connect with me on:

- https://www.shubhammishra.co.in
- https://twitter.com/shubmishra07
- https://www.facebook.com/shubhammishraofficial07
- https://www.instagram.com/shub7mishra
- https://www.linkedin.com/in/shubham-mishra07

About Shivangi Dwivedi

Shivangi Dwivedi is an accomplished Software Engineer with a keen interest and expertise in Quality Assurance. Having acquired a Bachelor's degree in Computer Science, she ventured into the world of software development and quality assurance. With over a year of experience in this field, she has developed a deep understanding of the importance of quality assurance in ensuring the smooth functioning of software systems. She has also gained proficiency in various quality assurance tools and techniques, making her a valuable asset to any software development team.

You can connect with me on:

- https://shivangidwivedi.co.in
- https://linkedin.com/in/shivangi-dwivedi-656386171

Who this book is for

This book is intended for anyone who wants to prepare for a job interview in the field of quality assurance, including software testers, quality assurance engineers, and quality assurance analysts. It is also suitable for those who want to improve their knowledge and understanding of quality assurance concepts and practices. The book provides a comprehensive collection of interview questions and answers, covering a wide range of topics related to quality assurance, which will help the readers to prepare effectively for their interviews.

I

Introduction

Quality assurance (QA) is a set of activities that are designed to ensure that a product or service meets certain quality standards. It involves establishing quality standards and processes, as well as implementing measures to detect and prevent defects or errors in the product or service. The goal of QA is to ensure that the final product or service meets the requirements of the customer and is delivered in a timely and cost-effective manner.

Chapter 1

Quality assurance is an essential aspect of software development, ensuring that the end product is functional, reliable, and meets the user's needs. To achieve this, organizations have to employ quality assurance experts who are responsible for overseeing the software development process and ensuring that each phase adheres to established standards and procedures. This Quality Assurance Interview Q&A book is designed to help both beginners and experienced quality assurance professionals prepare for interviews. The book covers a wide range of quality assurance topics, including software testing methodologies, test automation, and software development life cycle (SDLC) models.

The book provides an in-depth look at the most commonly asked interview questions and their best possible answers, covering everything from the basics of software testing to the most complex automation tools and techniques. Whether you are an entry-level QA professional or a seasoned expert, this book will help you brush up on your knowledge and prepare for any quality assurance interview.

In the following chapters, we will cover the essential topics and questions that you should be aware of to prepare for a quality assurance interview. The book is designed to be an easy-to-use reference guide for software quality assurance professionals, software developers, and anyone else involved in the software development process.

II

Quality Assurance

Quality Assurance (QA) refers to the systematic process of ensuring that a product or service meets the required quality standards. The primary objective of QA is to prevent errors and defects in the product development process. It involves planning, monitoring, controlling, and reporting all the activities necessary to ensure that the product or service meets the specified requirements. QA helps in identifying defects early in the development process, thereby reducing the cost of defect correction. It ensures that the product meets customer expectations, is delivered on time, and is of high quality. Overall, QA plays a crucial role in ensuring the success of any product or service.

Chapter 2

Testing shows the presence, not the absence of bugs.
– Edsger Dijkstra

Q1 Explain Quality Assurance?

Quality Assurance refers to the systematic process of monitoring, measuring, and evaluating products, services, or processes against established standards to ensure that they meet customer expectations and regulatory requirements. It aims to prevent defects, improve efficiency, and enhance customer satisfaction.

Q2 Explain how Quality Assurance (QA) is distinct from Software Testing?

Quality Assurance is a comprehensive process that encompasses all aspects of quality, including planning, designing, implementing, and monitoring.

Software testing, on the other hand, is a subset of Quality Assurance that focuses specifically on identifying and resolving defects in software applications.

Q3 What is the purpose of QA in Software Development?

The purpose of Quality Assurance (QA) in Software Development is to ensure that the software product meets the specified quality standards, customer requirements, and business objectives.

QA aims to prevent defects, identify and resolve issues in the early stages of the development process, improve the efficiency of the development process, and enhance customer satisfaction. It also involves creating and implementing quality standards, processes, and methodologies to ensure consistent and reliable product quality.

Q4 Explain the lifecycle of a Quality Assurance Process?

The lifecycle of a Quality Assurance (QA) process typically includes the following stages:

1. **Planning:** In this stage, the QA team identifies the quality standards and objectives, determines the testing methodologies and tools to be used, and defines the scope of the QA process.
2. **Design:** In this stage, the QA team develops test plans, test cases, and test scripts based on the requirements and specifications of the software product.
3. **Execution:** In this stage, the QA team executes the test cases and records the results. Any defects or issues identified are reported to the development team for resolution.
4. **Reporting:** In this stage, the QA team generates reports on the test results, defect reports, and other relevant metrics. These reports are used to evaluate the overall quality of the software product.
5. **Retesting:** In this stage, the QA team retests the software product after defects have been fixed to ensure that they have been resolved and that the product meets the required quality standards.
6. **Release:** In this stage, the software product is released to the market or

deployed to the production environment after it has passed all the quality checks and has met the specified quality standards.

7. **Monitoring:** In this stage, the QA team monitors the performance of the software product in the production environment to identify any defects or issues that may arise and to ensure that the product continues to meet the quality standards.

Q5 Explain the differences between Test Strategy and Test Plans?

A test plan outlines the detailed approach to testing a software application and typically includes test objectives, scope, resources, test cases, and schedules. It is a comprehensive document that provides a roadmap for the testing process.

A test strategy, on the other hand, is a high-level document that outlines the overall approach for testing a software application. It includes details such as testing methodologies, testing types, and the roles and responsibilities of the testing team. It provides a broad overview of the testing process.

Q6 Define Build and Release. Also, state the difference between them?

Build and Release are two related but distinct concepts in software development.

In software development, a build refers to compiling the source code into an executable or deployable format, which can be tested or released.

A release, on the other hand, refers to the process of making a build or a software version available to end users.

While a build is an intermediate step that focuses on the compilation of the code, a release is a final step that involves making the software available to the end users.

Q7 What are Bug Leakage and Bug Release?

Bug leakage occurs when a bug that was identified and reported during the testing phase goes unnoticed and reaches the production environment, causing issues for the end users. This can happen due to inadequate testing, poor communication, or other factors.

Bug release refers to the process of deliberately releasing a software version that contains known bugs. This may happen when a bug is considered a low priority or the release deadline is tight.

Q8 Define Monkey Testing?

Monkey testing, also known as random testing or ad-hoc testing, is a software testing technique that involves randomly testing the application with no specific test cases or plans. In this technique, the tester tries to break the application by performing random and unstructured actions such as clicking buttons, entering invalid data, and navigating through the application unpredictably.

Monkey testing can help identify defects or unexpected behavior that may not be discovered through other testing methods. However, it should not be used as a replacement for structured testing methods.

Q9 Explain Gorilla Testing?

Gorilla testing is a software testing technique that focuses on testing a specific module or feature of the software application intensively and extensively. It involves subjecting the module or feature to a variety of tests and scenarios to identify potential defects or issues.

Gorilla testing aims to ensure that the specific module or feature is stable, reliable, and performs as expected under different conditions. It is often used when a critical module or feature of the application is identified, and a high level of confidence in its performance is required.

Q10 What is Testware?

Testware refers to the artifacts created during the software testing process, including test plans, test cases, test scripts, test data, and test reports. It also includes the tools, utilities, and frameworks used for testing. Testware is an essential component of software testing as it helps ensure the quality and reliability of the software product.

Q11 What do you know about traceability matrix?

A traceability matrix is a document that maps and links the requirements or specifications of a software project to the test cases that verify those requirements. It provides a traceable link between the requirements, test cases, and defects, allowing the team to track the progress of testing and ensure that all requirements have been tested and met. It is a useful tool for managing and maintaining the quality of the software product.

Q12 Differentiate between Verification and Validation.

Verification and validation are two important concepts in software testing. Verification is the process of evaluating the software product or component to ensure that it meets the specified requirements and standards.

Validation, on the other hand, is the process of evaluating the software product to ensure that it meets the user's needs and expectations and that it solves the intended business problems. In other words, verification focuses on meeting technical requirements, while validation focuses on meeting business requirements.

Q13 State the difference between Retesting and Regression Testing?

Retesting and regression testing are two types of software testing that are used to ensure the quality and reliability of the software product.

Retesting is the process of testing a specific defect or issue that was previously identified and fixed. It is performed to ensure that the defect has been resolved and that the system functions as expected.

Regression testing, on the other hand, is the process of testing the entire system or application after changes or modifications have been made to ensure that the existing functionalities are not affected. It helps identify any new defects or issues that may have been introduced during the changes or modifications.

Q14 What do you know about Quality Audit?

A quality audit is a systematic and independent examination of a software project, process, or product to assess its compliance with the relevant standards, processes, and best practices.

The objective of a quality audit is to identify areas of improvement, provide feedback, and ensure that the software product or process meets the required quality standards. A quality audit can be internal or external and can be performed at different stages of the software development life cycle.

Q15 What is Defect Leakage Ratio?

Defect leakage ratio is a metric that measures the percentage of defects found during testing that are not identified and fixed before the software product is released to the end users.

Q16 Please provide an explanation of the various types of documentation used for Software Quality Assurance?

Software quality assurance documentation includes a variety of documents created during the software development process to ensure the quality of the software product. Here are some of the most common forms of software quality assurance documentation:

1. **Test plan:** A document that outlines the testing approach, test objectives, test strategies, and test schedules for the software project.
2. **Test cases:** A document that describes the test scenarios, inputs, and expected results for each test case.
3. **Test scripts:** A document that contains the step-by-step instructions for executing the test cases.
4. **Test report:** A document that provides an overview of the testing process, including the test results, defects, and other relevant metrics.
5. **Traceability matrix:** A document that maps the requirements to the corresponding test cases to ensure that all requirements have been tested.
6. **Defect report:** A document that records and tracks the defects identified during testing.
7. **Quality assurance plan:** A document that outlines the quality assurance approach, processes, and procedures for the software project.
8. Standards and procedures: A document that describes the coding standards, testing procedures, and other relevant guidelines for the software development team.
9. **Configuration management plan:** A document that outlines the processes and procedures for managing the software configuration, including version control and change management.

These documents are essential for ensuring that the software product is of high quality and meets the desired standards and requirements.

Q17 Can you describe the principle of Test Driven Development??

Test-driven development (TDD) is a software development approach where tests are written first before any code is written. The process typically involves the following steps:

1. **Write a test:** The developer writes a test case that specifies the expected behavior of the software.
2. **Run the test:** The test is executed, and it should fail since no code has been written yet.
3. **Write code:** The developer writes the code to make the test pass.
4. **Run the test:** The test is executed again, and it should pass if the code is correct.
5. **Refactor:** The developer refactors the code to improve its design and maintainability while ensuring that the tests continue to pass.

Q18 Could you state the primary objective of Test Driven Development?

TTD goal is to ensure that the code meets the required specifications and that any changes made to the code do not break existing functionality. TDD helps improve the quality of the software by ensuring that it is thoroughly tested and meets the required specifications.

Q19 Can you provide a definition of a Cause-Effect Graph?

Cause-Effect Graph is a graphical representation of the relationship between the inputs and outputs of a system or software module. It is also known as an Ishikawa diagram or fishbone diagram.

It helps in identifying the root cause of defects by breaking down the system into its different components and analyzing their relationships. The diagram includes different factors that contribute to a problem or defect and their interrelationships.

Q20 Could you explain the concept of Thread Testing?

Thread testing is a type of software testing that involves testing the behavior of multi-threaded applications or systems. It involves simulating multiple concurrent users or processes and verifying that the application behaves correctly and provides consistent results under different thread configurations and loads. The goal is to identify and prevent race conditions, deadlocks, and other issues that may arise in multi-threaded environments.

Q21 Can you list the five dimensions of risk?

The five dimensions of risk are as follows:

1. **Product risk:** It is the risk associated with the software product's quality and performance, including defects, errors, and other issues that may impact its functionality.
2. **Project risk:** It is the risk associated with the software development project's successful completion, including the risk of delays, budget overruns, and other project-related issues.
3. **Process risk:** It is the risk associated with the software development process, including the risk of deviations from established processes

and procedures, which may impact the quality and performance of the software.

4. **People risk:** It is the risk associated with the people involved in the software development process, including their skills, knowledge, and ability to perform their roles effectively.

5. **Business risk:** It is the risk associated with the software product's impact on the business, including the risk of financial loss, reputation damage, and other business-related issues.

Q22 Can you provide an explanation of Regression Testing?

Regression testing is a type of software testing that involves retesting a previously tested program to ensure that changes or enhancements to the software have not affected its existing functionality.

It helps to identify any defects or issues that may have been introduced due to the changes made to the software. The goal of regression testing is to ensure that the software continues to function as expected and remains stable and reliable.

Q23 What criteria should be used to select test cases for Regression Testing?

Regression testing aims to ensure that changes to the software do not have any unintended effects on the existing functionality. To achieve this, it is necessary to select the right test cases for regression testing. The following test cases should be selected for regression testing:

1. **Test cases related to the changed or modified code:** Test cases related to the changed or modified code should be selected for regression testing to ensure that the changes have not impacted the existing functionality.

2. **Test cases related to the impacted areas:** Test cases related to the

impacted areas of the software should be selected for regression testing to ensure that changes made to one area of the software do not affect the functionality of other areas.

3. **Critical test cases:** Critical test cases that are important for the software's overall functionality and user experience should be selected for regression testing.

4. **Test cases related to the frequently used features:** Test cases related to frequently used features should be selected for regression testing as these features are more likely to be impacted by changes to the software.

5. **Test cases related to the previously reported defects:** Test cases related to previously reported defects should be selected for regression testing to ensure that the fixes applied for those defects have not introduced any new issues.

Overall, the selection of test cases for regression testing should be based on the changes made to the software and the impact of those changes on the existing functionality.

Q24 Can you explain the difference between Severity and Priority?

Severity and priority are two important concepts in software testing and bug reporting, and they represent different aspects of a defect.

Severity refers to the impact of a defect on the software's functionality or performance. It is the degree of impact that the defect has on the system. The severity of a defect is often categorized as low, medium, or high, depending on the extent of its impact on the software.

Priority refers to the urgency with which a defect needs to be fixed. It is the importance of the defect concerning other defects and the project timeline. The priority of a defect is often categorized as low, medium, or high, depending on the urgency of fixing the defect.

In summary, severity describes the extent of the impact of a defect on the software, while priority describes the urgency with which the defect needs to be fixed. A high-severity defect may not necessarily have a high priority if it does not affect critical functionality or if it can be worked around, whereas a low-severity defect may have a high priority if it affects critical functionality or is blocking other work.

Q25 Could you describe the difference between Functional and Non-Functional Testing?

Functional testing and non-functional testing are two different types of software testing that are used to ensure the quality and performance of the software. The main differences between functional testing and non-functional testing are:

Functional Testing:

- Functional testing focuses on testing the individual functions of the software and verifying that they meet the specified requirements.
- It ensures that the software behaves as expected and performs the functions it was designed to perform.
- The goal of functional testing is to ensure that the software meets the functional requirements specified in the design and that it works correctly from a user's perspective.
- Examples of functional testing include unit testing, integration testing, system testing, and acceptance testing.

Non-Functional Testing:

- Non-functional testing focuses on testing the non-functional aspects of the software, such as performance, security, usability, reliability, and scalability.
- It ensures that the software meets the non-functional requirements

specified in the design, such as response time, throughput, and resource utilization.

- The goal of non-functional testing is to ensure that the software meets the quality attributes specified in the design and that it works correctly under different conditions.
- Examples of non-functional testing include performance testing, security testing, usability testing, reliability testing, and scalability testing.

In summary, functional testing ensures that the software works correctly from a user's perspective, while non-functional testing ensures that the software meets the quality attributes specified in the design. Both types of testing are important for ensuring the overall quality and performance of the software.

Q26 What factors should be considered to determine when to stop software testing?

The decision to stop testing is an important one that should be based on a variety of factors, including the project timeline, the quality goals, the level of testing performed, and the level of risk. Here are some factors to consider when deciding when to stop testing:

1. **Completion of test coverage:** Ensure that all the test cases planned have been executed and there is sufficient test coverage across different test scenarios.
2. **Bug closure rate:** Ensure that the bug closure rate is declining and that most of the high-priority bugs have been fixed and retested.
3. **Risk-based analysis:** Analyze the risk factors and identify critical areas that require more testing. Make sure that the most important functions or modules have been tested extensively and that the risk of critical defects is minimized.
4. **Time and budget constraints:** Consider the project timeline and budget, and ensure that testing has been performed within the allocated time and resources.

5. **User acceptance:** Consider user feedback, and ensure that the system meets user expectations and requirements.
6. **Stakeholder agreement:** Ensure that all stakeholders agree that sufficient testing has been performed and that the system is ready for release.

In summary, the decision to stop testing is based on a combination of factors, and a comprehensive risk-based analysis should be performed to ensure that sufficient testing has been performed and that the system is ready for release.

Q27 Can you distinguish between Load Testing and Stress Testing?

Load testing and stress testing are both types of performance testing used to evaluate how a system behaves under various conditions. The main differences between load testing and stress testing are:

Load Testing:

- Load testing is a type of performance testing that evaluates how a system performs under normal and expected load conditions.
- The goal of load testing is to determine the maximum operating capacity of the system, measure the response time, and ensure that the system can handle the expected user load without degradation.
- Load testing is typically done by gradually increasing the user load until the system reaches its maximum capacity, and then measuring the response time, throughput, and other performance metrics.

Stress Testing:

- Stress testing is a type of performance testing that evaluates how a system behaves under extreme load conditions, such as peak user loads or system failures.
- The goal of stress testing is to determine the system's stability and

reliability under extreme conditions and to identify any weaknesses in the system's architecture or design.

- Stress testing is typically done by overloading the system with more load than it can handle, and then observing how the system behaves, such as system crash or slow response time.

In summary, load testing is used to evaluate system performance under normal and expected load conditions, while stress testing is used to evaluate system performance under extreme conditions. Both types of testing are important for ensuring the quality and performance of the system.

Q28 Explain Ad-hoc Testing?

Ad-hoc testing is a type of software testing carried out without any specific plan or documentation in place. It is an informal approach to testing where the tester explores the application to find defects or issues that might not be discovered through other types of testing. Ad-hoc testing is typically performed by experienced testers who use their intuition, experience, and knowledge of the system to identify potential issues.

Q29 What are the differences between Ad-hoc Testing, Monkey Testing, and Exploratory Testing?

Ad-hoc testing, monkey testing, and exploratory testing are all informal approaches to software testing, but they differ in their methodology and purpose. Here are the main differences between these types of testing:

Ad-hoc testing:

- Ad-hoc testing is performed without any specific plan or documentation in place.
- The tester explores the application in an unstructured way, to find defects or issues that might not be discovered through other types of testing.

- Ad-hoc testing is typically performed by experienced testers who use their intuition, experience, and knowledge of the system to identify potential issues.

Monkey testing:

- Monkey testing is an informal approach to testing where the tester randomly clicks on buttons, links, and other UI elements to see if the system crashes or behaves unexpectedly.
- Monkey testing is often used in mobile application testing, where it can simulate user behavior and help identify issues related to device orientation, network connectivity, and other factors.
- Monkey testing is not a systematic approach to testing and is more focused on discovering unexpected behavior rather than verifying specific requirements.

Exploratory testing:

- Exploratory testing is an approach to testing where the tester combines testing, design, and learning in real time.
- The tester uses their experience and knowledge to design and execute test cases while exploring the application at the same time.
- The goal of exploratory testing is to discover defects, risks, and opportunities that might not be discovered through other types of testing.

In summary, ad-hoc testing is unstructured and performed without any specific plan, monkey testing is random and not systematic, and exploratory testing combines testing and learning in real time.

Q30 Explain Bug Life Cycle?

A bug life cycle, also known as a defect life cycle, is a process that describes the stages a defect goes through from the time it is discovered to the time it is resolved. The typical stages of a bug life cycle are:

1. **New:** When a defect is first discovered and reported, it is in the "new" stage.
2. **Assigned:** The defect is then assigned to a developer or a team for analysis and fixing.
3. **Open:** The developer begins to work on the defect and changes its status to "open."
4. **Fixed:** When the developer has fixed the defect, it is marked as "fixed."
5. **Verified:** The testing team then verifies that the defect has been fixed and changes its status to "verified."
6. **Closed:** If the defect has been fixed and verified, it is marked as "closed." If it cannot be reproduced or is not considered a defect, it may be marked as "rejected."
7. **Reopened:** If the defect is found again after it has been closed, it is marked as "reopened" and goes through the cycle again.

By following a bug life cycle, development and testing teams can manage defects more effectively, ensure they are resolved on time, and improve the overall quality of the software product.

Q31 Can you explain the concept of Bug/Defect Triage in Quality Assurance?

Bug/defect triage is the process of evaluating and prioritizing reported defects or issues based on their severity, impact on the system, and other factors. In this process, a cross-functional team including developers, testers, and project managers meets to review and discuss each issue and decide on the appropriate action, such as assigning it to a developer, scheduling it for a future release, or rejecting it. This helps to ensure that defects are resolved in a timely and efficient manner.

Q32 Can you explain Stubs and Drivers and distinguish between them?

Stubs and drivers are both types of software components used in testing, but they serve different purposes.

A driver is a software component that is used in testing modules that have dependencies on other modules or systems. It simulates the behavior of the dependent module or system to allow the module being tested to be executed and verified. A driver is used when the module being tested is incomplete and requires additional code to run.

On the other hand, a stub is a software component that is used in testing modules that have dependencies on other modules or systems. It simulates the behavior of the dependent module or system to allow the module being tested to be executed and verified. A stub is used when the module being tested is complete but the dependent module is not yet available.

In summary, drivers are used to simulate the behavior of the dependent module, while stubs are used to simulate the behavior of the module that is being depended upon.

III

Manual Testing

Manual testing is the process of identifying defects or errors in a software application manually, without the use of automated tools or scripts. It involves testing every feature of the software application to ensure that it meets the specified requirements and functions as expected. Manual testing is a crucial aspect of the software development lifecycle, and it helps to identify issues early on in the development process.

Chapter 3

Manual testing is like eating an elephant. You have to do it one bite at a time, but you'll get there eventually.

*- **Anonymous***

Q1 Can you provide a definition of Software Testing?

Software testing is a process of verifying and validating a software application to ensure that it is functioning as expected and meeting the requirements of the end users. It is done to identify any defects or bugs that may exist in the application and to ensure that it performs optimally, is reliable, and meets all necessary standards.

The testing process involves running the software application with different input data sets and conditions to ensure that it works correctly under all circumstances. Software testing is an essential part of the software development life cycle, and it helps to improve the quality and reliability of software applications.

Q2 What factors should be considered to determine when to conclude the testing process?

The decision to stop the testing process is based on multiple factors, including but not limited to:

1. **Test coverage:** Has the test coverage met the pre-defined criteria? If the testing team has covered all the test scenarios, then they can consider stopping the testing process.
2. **Time and budget constraints:** If the project timeline and budget are tight, the testing team may have to stop testing at a certain point to release the product within the deadline.
3. **Bug severity:** If critical defects are found, the testing process should continue until those are fixed and retested.
4. **Acceptance criteria:** If the product meets the acceptance criteria, the testing process can be stopped.
5. **Business needs:** Sometimes, external factors such as market conditions, customer needs, or business needs may require the testing process to be stopped.

Ultimately, the decision to stop the testing process is a tradeoff between the level of quality desired and the constraints imposed by the project, budget, and timelines. It is essential to document the decision-making process to ensure that the reasons for stopping the testing process are clear and transparent to all stakeholders involved.

Q3 What are the essential skills required to become a Software Tester?

To become a software tester, one needs a combination of technical and soft skills. Technical skills include knowledge of software development lifecycle, programming languages, databases, test automation tools, and bug-tracking systems. Soft skills include communication, teamwork, attention to detail, problem-solving, and critical thinking.

A tester must also be able to think creatively and understand end-users' needs to identify any issues with the software before it goes to production. Continuous learning and adaptability are also essential skills for a software tester, as technology and testing methodologies continue to evolve.

Q4 Can you explain Verification and Validation in Software Testing?

Verification and Validation are two important concepts in software testing.

Verification refers to the process of evaluating a software product or system to determine whether it meets the specified requirements and standards. This involves checking that the software is being built according to the design specifications, code standards, and requirements and that it meets the needs of the stakeholders. Verification helps ensure that the software product or system is of high quality, reliable, and performs as expected.

Validation, on the other hand, refers to the process of evaluating a software product or system to determine whether it meets the intended use and requirements of the end users. This involves checking that the software is fit for the purpose it was designed for and that it meets the needs of the users. Validation helps ensure that the software product or system meets the expectations and requirements of the end users.

Q5 Can you provide a definition of Static Testing and describe when it begins and what it covers?

Static testing is a technique used in software testing where the testing is performed without executing the code. This type of testing is usually done at an early stage of the software development life cycle (SDLC) to detect and fix defects and issues before the actual coding begins.

Static testing can be performed on various software artifacts such as requirement documents, design documents, source code, and test plans. It typically involves a thorough review of the artifacts to find issues related to syntax errors, logical errors, and adherence to coding standards and guidelines.

Static testing can be conducted in several ways, including reviews, walkthroughs, and inspections. It helps in improving the overall quality of the software by detecting and fixing defects early in the SDLC, thereby reducing the cost and time required to fix defects in the later stages of development.

Q6 Can you list the benefits of Manual Testing?

There are several advantages of manual testing, including:

1. **Exploratory testing:** Manual testing allows for exploratory testing, where testers can explore and discover new issues that automated tests may not catch.
2. **Flexibility:** Manual testing is more flexible than automated testing, as it allows testers to adapt to changing requirements and features.
3. **Cost-effective:** Manual testing can be more cost-effective for small projects, as it does not require expensive tools or resources.
4. **User perspective:** Manual testing can provide a better understanding of the user's perspective and user experience.
5. **Human judgment:** Manual testing allows testers to use their judgment and experience to identify potential issues that may not be captured by

automated testing.

6. **Ad hoc testing:** Manual testing allows for ad hoc testing, where testers can quickly test specific areas of an application without having to create formal test cases.

7. **Real-world scenarios:** Manual testing allows testers to test in real-world scenarios, where they can replicate how users would interact with an application more realistically.

Overall, manual testing can be a valuable complement to automated testing, as it provides a more comprehensive approach to testing software.

Q7 Define test case?

A test case is a set of conditions, instructions, or steps used to determine whether a software application, system, or feature is working as expected. It typically includes inputs, expected results, and actual results. A test case is designed to validate that a particular function or feature of a software application works correctly and meets the specified requirements.

Test cases are usually created based on the software requirements and are used to ensure that the software is reliable, functional, and meets the user's needs. The results of the test cases are documented and used to identify defects or errors in the software, which can then be corrected by developers.

Q8 Can you provide an explanation of SDLC?

SDLC (Software Development Life Cycle) is a process used by software development teams to design, develop, and test high-quality software. The SDLC process consists of several phases that are carried out in a specific order, including planning, analysis, design, implementation, testing, and maintenance.

Each phase has its own specific goals, activities, and deliverables that contribute to the overall success of the software development project. Following a well-defined SDLC process can help ensure that the software is of high quality, is delivered on time and within budget, and meets the needs of the end users.

Q9 Explain Black-box testing?

Black-box testing is a testing technique in which the tester doesn't have access to the internal structure or code of the software being tested. The tester focuses on the software's external behavior and functionality and tests the software by providing input and examining the output.

The goal of black-box testing is to ensure that the software meets its functional requirements and behaves correctly, regardless of its internal structure or implementation details. Black-box testing is commonly used in functional and acceptance testing and can be performed manually or through automated testing tools.

Q10 Can you provide a definition of Test Plan and describe what it typically includes?

A test plan is a document that outlines the approach, objectives, scope, and resources required for a testing project. It includes the details of the testing activities to be performed, the roles and responsibilities of the team members, the timelines for each testing activity, and the criteria for determining the success or failure of the testing.

A typical test plan includes the following sections:

1. **Introduction:** This section provides an overview of the testing project, its purpose, and the scope of the testing.
2. **Test strategy:** This section describes the approach, techniques, and tools that will be used for testing.
3. **Test objectives:** This section outlines the goals and objectives of the testing project, including what needs to be tested and how.

4. **Test schedule:** This section outlines the timelines and milestones for each testing activity.

5. **Test environment:** This section describes the hardware, software, and network configurations that will be used for testing.

6. **Test deliverables:** This section outlines the expected deliverables from the testing project, such as test plans, test cases, test scripts, and test reports.

7. **Test resources:** This section lists the personnel and resources required for testing, such as testers, developers, tools, and equipment.

8. **Test risks:** This section identifies the potential risks and issues that may arise during testing and outlines the contingency plans for addressing them.

9. **Test metrics:** This section outlines the metrics that will be used to measure the success of the testing project, such as defect density, defect removal efficiency, and test coverage.

10. **Approval:** This section outlines the approval process for the test plan and includes the signatures of the relevant stakeholders.

Q11 Explain test coverage?

Test coverage is a measure used to describe the degree to which the source code of a program has been tested. It is the technique of measuring what percentage of code lines, branches, statements, or conditions have been executed or tested. Test coverage is essential to ensure that the tests are comprehensive and that all code paths are tested.

The goal of test coverage is to ensure that all the critical functionalities of the software are tested and verified and to identify any parts of the code that have not been tested, which may be prone to defects. Test coverage can be measured using various techniques, such as code coverage, branch coverage, statement coverage, and path coverage.

The test coverage results can be used to improve the testing process and make sure that the software is fully functional and reliable.

Q12 Can you provide a definition of Test Scenario?

A test scenario is a high-level description of a specific functionality or feature of a software application that needs to be tested. It is a detailed description of a particular use case that outlines the steps, data inputs, and expected outputs to achieve specific objectives or outcomes.

Q13 Can you provide an explanation of whether achieving 100% Testing Coverage is feasible, and if so, how it can be ensured?

Achieving 100% testing coverage is practically impossible due to various factors such as time, resources, and the complexity of the system. However, it is important to strive for maximum coverage to ensure comprehensive testing of the system.

To ensure maximum coverage, the following approaches can be adopted:

1. **Prioritizing testing:** Testing should be prioritized based on the criticality of the features and functionality of the system. Critical and high-priority features should be tested thoroughly to ensure maximum coverage.
2. **Risk-based testing:** Risk-based testing involves identifying potential risks associated with the system and testing the areas that pose the highest risks. This helps to focus testing efforts on critical areas and ensure maximum coverage.
3. **Code coverage analysis:** Code coverage analysis is a technique that measures how much of the code has been executed during testing. This helps to identify areas of the code that have not been tested and ensure maximum coverage.
4. **Automation testing:** Automation testing can help increase testing coverage by automating repetitive and time-consuming tests. This ensures that tests are executed consistently and thoroughly.

By adopting these approaches, maximum testing coverage can be achieved, although it may not be possible to achieve 100% coverage

Q14 Explain Unit Testing?

Unit testing is a software testing technique that involves testing individual units or components of a software application in isolation from the rest of the system. The purpose of unit testing is to validate that each unit of the software performs as expected and meets the design specifications.

Q15 Define Integration Testing?

Integration testing is a software testing technique that tests the interactions between different components or modules of a software application to ensure that they function correctly together as a complete system. The objective of integration testing is to detect any defects or errors that occur when the components are integrated.

Q16 Can you provide an explanation of whether System Testing can be performed at any stage of the software development lifecycle?

System testing is typically performed after the completion of integration testing, as it requires a fully integrated system to test. However, in some cases, system testing can be performed concurrently with integration testing if certain components of the system are complete and stable enough to be tested as a whole.

It is important to note that the scope of system testing is typically broader than that of integration testing, as it aims to test the entire system's functionality and performance in a real-world environment.

Q17 What actions should be taken when a bug is discovered during the testing process?

When a bug is discovered during testing, the following steps can be taken:

1. **Report the bug:** The bug should be reported immediately to the development team or the designated person responsible for bug tracking.
2. **Reproduce the bug:** The tester should try to reproduce the bug, i.e., recreate the same steps that led to the error to make sure that it is consistent.
3. **Document the bug:** The tester should document the bug by writing a detailed report that includes information such as the steps that led to the bug, the expected behavior, the actual behavior, and any other relevant information.
4. **Prioritize the bug:** The bug should be prioritized based on its severity and impact on the system.
5. **Assign the bug:** The bug should be assigned to the appropriate developer or team for fixing.

6. **Retest the bug:** Once the bug has been fixed, the tester should retest it to ensure that the fix has resolved the issue.

7. **Close the bug:** If the bug is fixed and passes the retest, the tester can close the bug.

It is important to ensure that all bugs are reported and tracked to ensure that the system is functioning as expected and to improve the quality of the software product.

Q18 Can you explain how to test a product when the requirements are not yet finalized?

Testing a product before the requirements are finalized can be challenging, as there may be changes in the requirements that can affect the testing process. However, there are a few strategies that can be employed to ensure that testing is conducted effectively:

1. **Participate in requirement gathering:** Being involved in the requirement gathering process allows the testers to understand the requirements as they evolve. They can identify areas where clarification is needed and provide feedback to ensure that the requirements are testable.

2. **Use exploratory testing:** Exploratory testing is a technique where the tester explores the product without any specific test cases. This is useful when requirements are not finalized, as the tester can gain a better understanding of the product and identify potential issues that may not have been specified in the requirements.

3. **Use risk-based testing:** When requirements are not finalized, it may be difficult to create a comprehensive test plan. A risk-based approach can be used to prioritize testing based on the areas that are most critical to the product's success.

4. **Conduct frequent regression testing:** As requirements evolve, it is important to ensure that existing functionality continues to work as expected. Frequent regression testing can help identify any issues

introduced by changes in the requirements.

5. **Communicate with the development team:** Testers should maintain open communication with the development team to ensure that any changes in requirements are understood and accounted for in the testing process.

Q19 Explain the types of Functional Testing?

Several types of functional testing can be performed on software applications. Some of the common types include:

1. **Unit testing:** This is the testing of individual units or components of the software to ensure that they are working correctly.
2. **Integration testing:** This is the testing of how different components or modules of the software work together when they are integrated.
3. **System testing:** This is the testing of the entire system as a whole to ensure that it meets the functional requirements.
4. **Regression testing:** This is the testing that is performed after making changes to the software to ensure that the existing functionality is not affected.
5. **Acceptance testing:** This is the testing that is performed to ensure that the software meets the user's requirements and is ready for deployment.
6. **User acceptance testing (UAT):** This is the testing that is performed by the end-users or the stakeholders to ensure that the software meets their needs and requirements.
7. **Smoke testing:** This is the testing that is performed to ensure that the basic functionality of the software is working fine, and the system is stable enough to undergo further testing.
8. **Exploratory testing:** This is the testing that is performed without any predefined test cases or scripts, where testers try to identify defects in the software by exploring the application's features.
9. **Usability testing:** This is the testing that is performed to ensure that the software is user-friendly and that the end-users can easily use the

application without any difficulty.

Q20 Can you explain what White Box Testing is, and what are the different techniques used in it?

White box testing is a type of software testing that involves checking the internal logic, structure, and code of an application or system. In white box testing, the tester has access to the internal workings of the software and can look at the code and make informed decisions about where to focus testing efforts.

Some of the techniques used in white box testing include:

1. **Statement coverage:** This technique involves testing each statement in the code to ensure that it is executed at least once.
2. **Branch coverage:** This technique involves testing each possible branch in the code to ensure that all possible outcomes are covered.
3. **Condition coverage:** This technique involves testing each possible condition within a decision to ensure that all possible outcomes are covered.
4. **Path coverage:** This technique involves testing all possible paths through the code to ensure that all possible combinations of inputs and outputs are covered.
5. **Loop coverage:** This technique involves testing all possible iterations of a loop to ensure that it is executed the correct number of times and that all possible outcomes are covered.

White box testing is often used in conjunction with black box testing to ensure comprehensive testing of a software application or system.

Q21 Explain STLC?

STLC stands for Software Testing Life Cycle. It is a sequence of phases that a software product undergoes during its testing phase. The STLC is similar to the software development life cycle (SDLC) but focuses only on the testing phase of the product.

The STLC typically consists of six phases:

1. **Requirement Analysis:** In this phase, the testing team reviews and analyzes the requirements of the software to ensure that they are clear, complete, and testable.
2. **Test Planning:** In this phase, the testing team creates a test plan that outlines the testing approach, testing strategy, test objectives, and test schedule.
3. **Test Design:** In this phase, the testing team develops test cases based on the requirements and test plan.
4. **Test Execution:** In this phase, the testing team executes the test cases and records the test results.
5. **Test Reporting:** In this phase, the testing team prepares test reports that summarize the testing results and the status of the defects.
6. **Test Closure:** In this phase, the testing team reviews the testing process and the test results to determine if the testing objectives were met. The team also prepares the final test report and archives the testing artifacts.

The STLC ensures that the software product is thoroughly tested and meets the quality standards before it is released to the end users.

Q22 What do you know about Sanity testing?

Sanity testing is a type of software testing that is performed after a software build to determine whether the build is stable enough for further testing. It is a basic level of testing that checks whether the major functionalities of the software are working as expected and whether the critical features are not broken.

It is also known as a subset of regression testing and is used to avoid wastage of time and resources during further testing phases if the build is unstable. Sanity testing helps to ensure that the software is ready for further testing and eventual release.

Q23 Can you explain the difference between Defects, Errors, and Bugs in the context of software development and testing?

In software testing, the terms "defects," "errors," and "bugs" are often used interchangeably, but there are some differences between them:

1. **Error:** An error is a human action that produces an incorrect or unexpected result. For example, if a programmer mistakenly enters a wrong formula in a code, that would be an error.
2. **Defect:** A defect is a flaw or deviation from the requirement or expected behavior of the software. It is a mistake that occurs during the development phase, and it is identified by testing. A defect can result from an error, but it can also be caused by other factors such as incorrect assumptions, misunderstandings, or miscommunication.
3. **Bug:** A bug is a defect that causes the software to malfunction, behave unexpectedly, or crash. It is a defect that is detected during the testing phase or after the software is released to the end-users. The term "bug" is often used to refer to any software problem, but technically, it refers only to defects that cause the software to fail or behave abnormally.

In summary, an error is a mistake made during coding, a defect is a deviation from the requirement, and a bug is a defect that causes the software to fail or behave unexpectedly.

Q24 Name four different test levels

The four different test levels are:

1. Unit testing
2. Integration testing
3. System testing
4. Acceptance testing

Q25 Explain GUI Testing?

GUI testing, also known as Graphical User Interface testing, is a type of software testing that checks the functionality, usability, and consistency of the graphical user interface of an application.

GUI testing involves testing the application's interface components such as menus, buttons, icons, text fields, and all other graphical elements that allow users to interact with the software.

The main goal of GUI testing is to ensure that the user interface of the application meets the design and usability requirements and that users can navigate and perform actions on the interface smoothly and efficiently.

Q26 Can you explain what the Top-Down and Bottom-Up approaches are in the context of software testing?

In software testing, a top-down approach is a testing approach that starts testing from the highest level of the software and works downwards, whereas the bottom-up approach is a testing approach that starts testing from the lowest level of the software and works upwards.

The top-down approach is also known as the "Big Bang" approach, as it starts with the testing of the system as a whole, and then moves to the lower levels. The top-down approach is useful when there is a clear and complete understanding of the system's requirements and architecture.

On the other hand, the bottom-up approach is also known as the "Incremental" approach, as it starts with the testing of individual modules or units and then integrates them one by one to test the system as a whole. The bottom-up approach is useful when the system's requirements and architecture are not well-defined or there is uncertainty in the system's behavior.

Both approaches have their advantages and disadvantages, and the selection of a particular approach depends on the system's requirements, architecture, and the testing team's expertise.

Q27 Explain test closure?

Test closure is the final stage of the software testing process. It involves the formal completion of testing after ensuring that all the test cases have been executed, all the bugs have been identified and fixed, and the software has met all the requirements.

The test closure phase includes activities such as test summary reports, lessons learned reports, test artifacts handover, and releasing the test environment. This phase provides a comprehensive report of the software testing effort and helps to assess the quality of the product.

Q28 What is Defect Removal Efficiency (DRE) in software testing?

Defect removal efficiency (DRE) is a metric used in software testing to measure the effectiveness of defect removal during the testing process. It is calculated by dividing the total number of defects found and fixed before release by the total number of defects found during the entire testing process. A higher DRE indicates that more defects have been identified and removed during testing.

Q29 Can you explain what the term "average age of a defect" means in software testing?

The average age of a defect in software testing is difficult to determine as it can vary depending on various factors, such as the complexity of the software, the testing approach, the severity of the defect, the resources available for fixing the defect, and more.

However, it is generally recommended to find and fix defects as early as possible in the software development life cycle to reduce the cost and effort required to fix them later.

Q30 Explain what Silk Test is and what its benefits are?

Silk Test is a functional testing tool used for regression and system testing of web-based and client-server applications. It is a tool provided by Micro Focus that allows for easy scripting of tests, and it provides support for multiple programming languages such as C++, .NET, Java, and others.

Silk Test also offers built-in debugging tools and supports object-oriented programming, which enables users to reuse code and increase efficiency in test automation. Additionally, it provides extensive reporting and analysis features, making it a popular choice for testing large and complex applications.

Q31 What are the essential components that should be included while drafting a bug report?

There are several key elements to consider while writing a bug report, including:

1. **Title/Summary:** A brief and clear summary of the bug or issue, which helps to quickly identify the problem.
2. **Description:** A detailed description of the issue, including steps to reproduce the problem, environment details, and any other relevant information.
3. **Severity/Priority:** An assessment of how severe the issue is and how much it impacts the functionality of the software. Priority indicates how soon the issue needs to be resolved.
4. **Expected result:** A clear description of what should happen when the software is functioning correctly.
5. **Actual result:** A clear description of what happened when the issue occurred.
6. **Attachments:** Screenshots, videos, or any other relevant files that can help to demonstrate the issue.
7. **Reproducibility:** Information on how often the issue can be reproduced and under what conditions.
8. **Test environment:** Details of the testing environment, such as operating system, browser, and hardware configurations.
9. **Date/time:** The date and time when the issue was observed.
10. **Assigned to:** The person responsible for fixing the issue or further investigation.
11. **Status:** The current status of the issue, whether it is open, closed, or in progress.
12. **Comments:** Any additional information or comments related to the issue that may be useful in resolving the problem.

By including all of these elements in a bug report, it becomes easier for developers and testers to understand and resolve the issue quickly and efficiently.

Q32 Explain Exploratory Testing?

Exploratory testing is an approach to software testing that is based on exploration and discovery. Instead of relying on pre-defined test cases and scripts, the tester designs and executes test cases in real time based on their intuition, expertise, and experience with the system under test. This approach is useful for finding unexpected bugs and improving overall test coverage.

Q33 Explain the term "Critical Bug"?

A critical bug is a type of software bug that has the most severe impact on the software system's functionality or performance. It can cause complete system failure, data loss, security breaches, or other significant issues that can affect the software's ability to function as intended. Critical bugs are considered the most severe type of bug, and their resolution is usually given the highest priority in the software development and testing process.

Q34 What is latent defect?

A latent defect is a type of software bug that is not detectable at the time of testing, but it can manifest later during the software lifecycle. These defects remain in the codebase and may arise due to incorrect coding, incomplete testing, or changing software requirements.

Latent defects can cause severe issues in the software system and can only be detected during real-world usage or by thorough testing at a later stage. Therefore, detecting and fixing these defects is crucial to maintain software quality and reliability.

Q35 Explain Acceptance Testing?

Acceptance testing is a software testing technique that determines if a software system meets the acceptance criteria of the customer or end-users. It is the final stage of the software testing process that is performed after the functional, integration, and system testing.

The purpose of acceptance testing is to validate whether the software is ready for delivery and can be accepted by the customer. It ensures that the software meets the requirements and specifications of the client and performs as expected.

Q36 Can you explain what is meant by Test comparators in software testing?

Test comparators are software tools used in automated testing to compare the actual results of a test with the expected results. These tools analyze the differences between the actual and expected outputs and provide detailed reports. Test comparators are useful in detecting bugs and errors in the software being tested.

They also help identify inconsistencies in the test results and can be used to improve the accuracy and efficiency of the testing process. Some popular test comparators used in automated testing include Apache JMeter, HP Unified Functional Testing (UFT), and Selenium.

Q37 In what scenarios would you opt for automated testing instead of manual testing?

There are several cases where choosing automated testing over manual testing may be considered:

1. **Repetitive Tasks:** Automated testing is a good choice for repetitive tasks, such as regression testing, where the same test cases need to be executed repeatedly.
2. **Large-Scale Testing:** Automated testing is well-suited for large-scale testing, where manual testing may be too time-consuming and expensive.
3. **Time Constraints:** Automated testing can save time and improve efficiency, especially when there are tight project timelines.
4. **High-Risk Scenarios:** Automated testing is a good option for high-risk scenarios, where manual testing may not be practical or safe, such as testing in hazardous environments or with dangerous equipment.
5. **Consistency:** Automated testing ensures consistency in testing, as the same test cases are executed in the same way every time.
6. **Accuracy:** Automated testing can reduce the chance of human error, ensuring that tests are executed accurately and consistently.
7. **Performance Testing:** Automated testing is a good choice for performance testing, where it is important to simulate heavy loads and measure response times.
8. **Resource Constraints:** Automated testing can be a good choice when there are resource constraints, such as a limited number of testers, as it can help to improve testing efficiency and coverage.

Q38 What is the reason behind boundary value analysis being an effective technique for generating good test cases?

Boundary value analysis provides good test cases because it covers both valid and invalid inputs. For example, if an input field accepts values between 1 and 100, the boundary values would be 1, 100, and values just below and above them, such as 0, 101, and 99. Boundary value analysis would test all these values and ensure that the program handles them correctly. This technique is effective in identifying defects that may occur at the limits of the input range and can help improve the reliability and accuracy of the software.

IV

Automated Testing

Automated testing refers to the use of software tools to execute tests, assess the results, and compare them with the expected outcomes. It involves writing scripts or codes to automate the manual testing process, which saves time and effort while increasing accuracy and coverage. Automated testing is often used for repetitive, time-consuming, or complex test cases that are difficult to perform manually. It can also detect defects early in the software development life cycle, reducing the cost and effort required to fix them later. Automated testing tools include unit testing frameworks, GUI testing tools, and performance testing tools, among others.

Chapter 4

Automation does not mean intelligent automation. You still need smart people to figure out what to automate.

- Scott W. Ambler

Q1 What are the differences between manual testing and automated testing?

Manual testing and automated testing are two different approaches to software testing, with their advantages and limitations.

Manual testing is the process of manually executing test cases, checking the software application's behavior, and recording the results. Manual testing requires human intervention to test the software, and it is done manually by a testing team. It is usually performed in the early stages of the software development life cycle (SDLC) and can be time-consuming and labor-intensive.

Automated testing, on the other hand, is the use of specialized software tools to execute tests and compare actual outcomes with expected outcomes. Automated testing requires less human intervention and can be executed faster than manual testing. It is often used in the later stages of the SDLC, especially for regression testing, performance testing, and load testing.

The main differences between manual and automated testing are:

- Manual testing requires human intervention, while automated testing is performed by software tools.
- Manual testing is time-consuming and labor-intensive, while automated testing is faster and can be executed repeatedly.
- Manual testing is suitable for exploratory testing, while automated testing is better suited for regression testing, performance testing, and load testing.
- Manual testing is more flexible and adaptable, while automated testing is more precise and repeatable.

Both manual and automated testing is essential for delivering high-quality software, and they complement each other. Manual testing is suitable for exploratory testing, usability testing, and ad-hoc testing, while automated testing is ideal for regression testing, load testing, and performance testing.

Q2 What are the factors to be considered when choosing an automated testing tool or framework?

When selecting an automated testing tool or framework, there are several factors to consider:

1. **Compatibility:** The tool or framework should be compatible with the technology, platform, and programming language used to develop the software application.
2. **Ease of use:** The tool or framework should be easy to use, even for non-technical team members.
3. **Functionality:** The tool or framework should provide the required functionality, such as support for different types of testing, reporting, and integration with other tools.
4. **Customization:** The tool or framework should be customizable to meet specific testing needs.

5. **Support:** The tool or framework should have a good support system, such as documentation, tutorials, and customer support.
6. **Cost:** The cost of the tool or framework should be reasonable and within the budget.
7. **Scalability:** The tool or framework should be able to scale to support larger and more complex applications.
8. **Integration:** The tool or framework should be able to integrate with other tools used in the software development process, such as CI/CD tools and bug tracking tools.
9. **Community:** The tool or framework should have an active and supportive community of users who can provide assistance and share knowledge.
10. **Security:** The tool or framework should be secure and should not pose a security risk to the software application.

Q3 Is it necessary to automate all types of testing?

No, you should not automate all testing. While automation can be beneficial in many cases, there are situations where manual testing may be more appropriate or effective. Here are some factors to consider when deciding whether to automate testing:

1. **Frequency of testing:** If a particular test needs to be run frequently or repeatedly, it may be more efficient to automate it.
2. **Complexity of testing:** If a test involves a large amount of data or complex scenarios, automation can help ensure consistency and accuracy.
3. **Stability of the application:** If the application is not yet stable and is undergoing frequent changes, it may be more effective to focus on manual testing until the application stabilizes.
4. **Cost and time constraints:** Automating testing can be expensive and time-consuming, so it's important to weigh the costs and benefits of automation against manual testing.
5. **User interface testing:** User interface testing can be difficult to automate, so it may be more effective to conduct these tests manually.

6. **Exploratory testing:** Exploratory testing involves exploring the application to find defects and potential issues, which may be difficult to automate.

In summary, while automation can be beneficial in many cases, it's important to evaluate each test case and determine whether automation is the best approach based on the specific requirements and constraints of the project.

Q4 What are the different areas where automation testing can be applied?

Several areas of software testing can be automated, including:

1. **Unit testing:** This involves testing individual components or modules of the software to ensure that they function correctly in isolation.
2. **Functional testing:** This involves testing the software's features and functionality to ensure that they meet the requirements and specifications.
3. **Regression testing:** This involves testing the software to ensure that changes or updates to the code have not introduced new defects or broken existing functionality.
4. **Performance testing:** This involves testing the software's performance under various conditions to ensure that it can handle the expected workload and user traffic.
5. **Security testing:** This involves testing the software's security features to ensure that they are robust and protect against potential threats.
6. **Integration testing:** This involves testing the software's interactions with other systems or components to ensure that they work together seamlessly.
7. **API testing:** This involves testing the software's APIs to ensure that they function correctly and integrate smoothly with other systems or components.

In summary, automation can be applied to many areas of software testing, and it's important to identify the most appropriate areas for automation based on the specific requirements and constraints of the project.

Q5 Which types of test cases are suitable for automation?

Not all test cases are suitable for automation. Test cases that are repetitive, time-consuming, or difficult to execute manually are good candidates for automation. Additionally, test cases that require multiple data sets, complex business logic, or frequent regression testing can also benefit from automation.

Here are some types of test cases that are often automated:

1. **Regression tests:** These test cases are executed to verify that the new changes do not break the existing functionality of the software.
2. **Performance tests:** These test cases are used to check the performance of the software under different load conditions.
3. **Smoke tests:** These test cases are executed to ensure that the basic functionality of the software is working after each build.
4. **Data-driven tests:** These test cases use different sets of test data to verify that the software works correctly under different conditions.
5. **GUI tests:** These test cases check the user interface of the software to ensure that it is working as expected.

It's important to keep in mind that not all test cases can be automated, and the decision to automate a test case should be based on factors such as the cost of automation, the frequency of execution, and the complexity of the test case.

Q6 Is it feasible to automate 100% of your processes?

No, it is not practical to automate 100% of testing processes. Some aspects of testing, such as exploratory testing, require human intuition and creativity. Additionally, some tests may be too complex or not cost-effective to automate. A balance between manual and automated testing is necessary to ensure comprehensive testing while maximizing efficiency.

Q7 How do I approach adding automation to my project, which presently lacks any automation?

Adding automation to a project can be a significant undertaking, but the following steps can help guide you:

1. **Evaluate the current testing process:** Identify the testing activities that could benefit from automation and assess the current testing process's strengths and weaknesses.
2. **Define the scope:** Determine which areas of testing can and should be automated, and establish clear goals and objectives for the automation effort.
3. **Choose appropriate tools:** Research and select the right automation tools and frameworks that meet the project's requirements and technical specifications.
4. **Create an automation plan:** Develop a comprehensive automation plan, including test cases to be automated, test data, test environment, and automation scripts.
5. **Implement and execute the automation:** Create and execute the automation scripts, debugging as necessary and making necessary adjustments.
6. **Evaluate the results:** Evaluate the effectiveness and efficiency of the automated testing by analyzing the results and identifying any areas for improvement.
7. **Maintain and update the automation:** Regularly maintain and update the automation scripts to ensure their relevance and effectiveness over

time.

It is important to note that automation is not a one-time activity, and it requires ongoing investment and maintenance to provide long-term benefits.

Q8 Can you explain what an automation testing framework is?

An automation testing framework is a set of guidelines, standards, and rules for automating software testing tasks. It provides a systematic approach to writing, managing, and executing automated test scripts. The framework includes components such as libraries, drivers, scripts, and test data, that help automate and streamline the testing process.

Q9 What distinguishes a good framework from a bad one?

A good automation testing framework is designed to be reusable, scalable, and maintainable. It should provide a clear separation of concerns between different components, be easy to understand and use and have good documentation. A good framework also supports multiple platforms, technologies, and testing types.

On the other hand, a bad framework is usually inflexible, difficult to maintain, and hard to use. It may have poor documentation, lack features, or use outdated technologies. A bad framework may also be overly complex or rely on a single technology or platform, making it difficult to scale or adapt to new requirements.

Q10 Is it essential to have a framework for automation testing?

No, frameworks are not necessary for automation. However, using a framework can help automate tests more efficiently and effectively by providing structure, organization, and reusable components.

Q11 Can you explain the different types of automation testing frameworks?

Yes, there are several types of automation testing frameworks, including:

1. **Linear Framework:** A simple, sequential test script where the testing steps are executed one after another.
2. **Modular Framework:** A framework where the test cases are divided into modules or functions, which are called by the main script.
3. **Data-Driven Framework:** A framework that uses external data sources to execute the same test script with multiple sets of test data.
4. **Keyword Driven Framework:** A framework that uses keywords to define the test steps and actions, making test scripts easier to understand and maintain.
5. **Hybrid Framework:** A combination of two or more frameworks that combines their strengths to create a more efficient and effective automation testing framework.
6. **Behavior-Driven Development (BDD) Framework:** A framework that uses a common language to describe the expected behavior of an application, making it easier for developers and testers to collaborate and write more effective tests.
7. **Test Driven Development (TDD) Framework:** A framework where developers write test cases before writing code, which ensures the code is developed to meet the specified requirements.

Q12 Are there any best practices for coding that you could offer while automating?

Yes, here are some good coding practices to follow while automating:

1. **Use meaningful names:** Use descriptive and meaningful names for functions, variables, and classes to improve readability and understanding.
2. **Use proper indentation and formatting:** Properly indent and format your code to improve readability and maintainability.
3. **Write modular code:** Write code in small modules, each responsible for a specific functionality, which makes it easier to maintain and modify the code.
4. **Use comments:** Use comments to explain the functionality of the code, making it easier for other team members to understand and modify the code.
5. **Use exception handling:** Use exception handling to handle errors and unexpected events in your code.
6. **Use object-oriented programming (OOP) concepts:** Use OOP concepts like inheritance, encapsulation, and abstraction to make your code reusable, modular, and scalable.
7. **Write reusable code:** Write reusable code by using functions, classes, and libraries to avoid duplicating code.
8. **Use version control:** Use version control to keep track of changes to your code and work collaboratively with other team members.

Following these practices can help you write clean, maintainable, and scalable automation code.

Q13 Are there any types of tests that you believe should not be automated?

Yes, some tests may not be suitable for automation. For example, tests that are highly dependent on user interaction or visual confirmation may not be suitable for automation. Similarly, tests that require complex data setup or involve complex calculations may not be feasible for automation. It's important to assess each test case and determine if it can be automated efficiently and effectively.

Q14 Is it appropriate to restrict testing to only UI testing?

No, testing should not be limited to UI testing. There are other types of testing, such as API testing, performance testing, security testing, and database testing, that are also important to ensure the quality of the software

Q15 What are the factors that can hinder testers from automating, and how can they be addressed?

Yes, there are a few factors that can hold testers back from automating, such as a lack of programming skills, limited resources, lack of management support, and resistance to change.

To overcome these barriers, testers can:

1. Focus on learning and improving their programming skills by attending training and practicing coding.
2. Make a strong business case for automation and seek management support for automation initiatives.
3. Use open-source tools to reduce the cost of automation.
4. Communicate the benefits of automation to other stakeholders and get them involved in the automation process.
5. Start with small automation projects and gradually expand the scope of automation over time.

Q16 Can you explain the key elements of an automation testing framework?

The main components of an automation testing framework are:

1. **Test scripts:** These are the actual test cases that need to be executed automatically.
2. **Test data:** It is the input data used for the test cases.
3. **Test environment:** It includes hardware, software, and network configurations needed for the test execution.
4. **Test execution engine:** It is responsible for executing the test cases and generating reports.
5. **Reporting:** It is used for capturing and reporting the test results.
6. **Test management:** It includes test planning, test case design, and test case management.
7. **Test automation tools:** These are used for developing and maintaining automation scripts.
8. **Configuration management:** It includes version control and maintaining the history of changes made to the test scripts.
9. **Error handling and recovery:** It involves handling any errors or failures encountered during the test execution and recovering from them.

Q17 Can you provide a description of some tools used for automating testing?

There are several tools available in the market for automating testing, some of which are:

1. **Selenium:** A popular open-source automation testing tool that supports multiple programming languages, browsers, and operating systems.
2. **Appium:** A cross-platform mobile automation testing tool that supports both iOS and Android platforms.
3. **TestComplete:** A comprehensive testing tool that supports various

testing types, including functional, regression, and load testing.

4. **JMeter:** A Java-based open-source tool for load testing that can simulate a heavy load on a server, network, or object to check its performance under different load conditions.

5. **Cucumber:** A tool that supports behavior-driven development (BDD) and allows collaboration between developers, testers, and business stakeholders.

6. **Jenkins:** An open-source automation server that helps to automate the build, test, and deployment process.

7. **Postman:** A tool that simplifies API testing by allowing testers to test, document, and share API endpoints.

8. **Robot Framework:** A generic test automation framework that supports multiple test libraries and can be extended with additional libraries.

These tools offer different features and functionalities, and the choice of tool depends on the specific requirements of the project

Q18 What are the different categories of testing frameworks?

Testing frameworks can be categorized into four types: linear scripting, modular, data-driven, and keyword-driven.

- Linear scripting frameworks run tests in sequential order.
- Modular frameworks divide tests into small and independent modules.
- Data-driven frameworks use test data stored in external files to execute tests.
- Keyword-driven frameworks use keywords to identify test actions.

Q19 Is automation testing valuable in agile methodologies?

Yes, automation testing can be very useful in agile methodologies. It is often a key component of agile testing. Automated tests can help speed up the testing process, allowing for more frequent and rapid feedback on the status of the software being developed. This is particularly important in agile methodologies, where there is a focus on continuous delivery and frequent releases.

Additionally, automated tests can help ensure that new features or changes to the software do not break existing functionality, which is crucial in agile development where changes are made frequently.

Q20 What approach you would take to automate the basic login functionality tests?

Automating basic login functionality tests can be approached using different methods. One of the most common ways is to utilize a testing tool like Selenium, which allows for the automation of web browser interactions.

Another method is to use a headless browser such as PhantomJS, which mimics a real browser but doesn't show anything on the screen, making it ideal for testing web applications.

When testing basic login functionality, tools like cURL or HTTPie can be used to make direct HTTP requests to the login page and check the responses. However, for testing advanced login functionality such as handling incorrect passwords or two-factor authentication, more comprehensive tools like Selenium or PhantomJS are needed.

Automating basic login functionality tests is generally feasible with the right tools and approach. However, the complexity of the login functionality can affect the difficulty level of the automation. With sufficient effort and the use of appropriate tools, it is possible to automate the most basic login functionality tests.

Q21 Is automation testing considered more of a black-box or white-box testing approach?

Automation testing can be both black-box testing and white-box testing depending on the level of access and knowledge of the tester to the internal workings of the system.

In black-box testing, the tester does not have any knowledge of the internal workings of the system and only interacts with the system through the user interface. In this case, automation testing can be considered black-box testing.

In white-box testing, the tester has access to the internal workings of the system and can write tests that interact with the system at the code level. In this case, automation testing can be considered white-box testing.

Overall, automation testing can be used in both black-box and white-box testing depending on the level of access and knowledge the tester has of the system.

Q22 How many test cases can you automate per day?

It's difficult to give a precise answer as the number of test cases that can be automated per day varies depending on various factors. Some of these factors include the complexity of the test cases, the automation tool being used, and the tester's level of expertise. On average, a tester can automate anywhere from 5 to 15 test cases per day. However, it's important to prioritize quality over quantity to ensure that the tests are effective and reliable.

Q23 Can you explain the process of the Automation Testing Life Cycle?

The Automation Testing Life Cycle (ATLC) is a set of steps that outlines the process of creating and executing automated test scripts. Here are the typical steps in the ATLC:

1. **Test Planning:** In this stage, the testing team identifies what needs to be automated and what tools and frameworks will be used.
2. **Test Design:** This stage involves designing the test cases and creating the test scripts.
3. **Test Development:** In this stage, the automated test scripts are created using the selected automation tool.
4. **Test Execution:** The automated test scripts are executed and the results are recorded.
5. **Test Maintenance:** Any changes to the application or its environment will require updates to the automated test scripts, which are made in this stage.
6. **Retesting:** When a defect is found and fixed, the automated test script is re-run to ensure that the issue has been resolved.
7. **Regression Testing:** In this stage, all automated test cases are re-executed to ensure that the changes made in the application have not introduced any new defects.
8. **Reporting:** The results of the automated tests are recorded and reported to the stakeholders.

By following these steps, the ATLC helps ensure that the automated testing process is organized, efficient, and effective.

Q24 What do you know about automated test script?

An automated test script is a program that performs a predefined set of actions on an application or system under test and verifies whether the expected results are obtained. These scripts are written using automation tools and can be executed repeatedly to check if the application or system is functioning as expected.

Q25 What is the test automation pyramid?

The test automation pyramid is a model that describes the ideal distribution of test automation in a software testing strategy. It is composed of three layers:

1. **Unit tests**: These are the lowest level of automated tests, and they test individual units of code in isolation. They are typically created by developers using unit testing frameworks like JUnit, NUnit, or pytest.
2. **Service tests**: These tests verify the interactions between different services or components within an application. They test the API layer of the application and can be created using tools like REST Assured, SoapUI, or Postman.
3. **UI tests**: These are the highest level of automated tests, and they test the application from a user's perspective. They interact with the application's user interface and can be created using tools like Selenium, Appium, or TestComplete.

The pyramid shape indicates that the bulk of the testing effort should be focused on unit and service tests, with fewer UI tests. This is because unit and service tests are faster, more reliable, and easier to maintain than UI tests. By following this model, teams can achieve faster feedback on changes and catch more issues earlier in the development process.

Q26 Should automation testing be the responsibility of developers or QA?

Both developers and QA engineers can be responsible for automating tests, depending on the organization's structure and processes. In some organizations, developers are responsible for writing automated tests as part of their coding process, while in others, QA engineers may be responsible for developing and maintaining the automation framework and writing test scripts. Ultimately, it is up to the organization to determine the roles and responsibilities for test automation based on their specific needs and goals.

Q27 What are the potential risks associated with automated testing?

Automated testing can also come with its own set of risks, which include:

1. **False sense of security:** Automated tests can give a false sense of security if they are not designed or executed properly. Testers may rely too heavily on automated tests and neglect manual testing, leading to overlooked defects.
2. **High maintenance:** Automated tests require regular maintenance to keep them up-to-date with changes in the application under test. This can become a significant burden if not managed properly.
3. **False positives:** Automated tests can also produce false positive results, indicating a defect where there is none. This can lead to wasted time and resources investigating non-existent issues.
4. **Limited scope:** Automated tests can only test what they are programmed to test, which means they may not catch certain types of defects. This can create blind spots in the testing process and leave important issues undetected.
5. **Cost:** Automated testing can be expensive to set up and maintain, particularly if the tools used require licensing fees or specialized skills.

It's important to weigh the benefits and risks of automation and determine whether it makes sense for your specific project and goals.

Q28 Have you used any object mapping tools such as QTP or UFT in the past? What was your experience with them?

Yes, Object mapping tools like QTP and UFT are generally considered to be very helpful in automating testing processes for web-based applications. These tools make it easier to identify elements on a web page, such as buttons, input fields, and links, which can be interacted with during testing. This, in turn, can help to save time and effort when writing test scripts and ensure that testing is more accurate and thorough.

Additionally, object mapping tools are also useful for identifying any changes or updates that have been made to the web application, which can help in performing regression testing. Overall, object mapping tools are a valuable addition to the testing toolkit and can greatly enhance the effectiveness and efficiency of testing processes.

Q29 What is a test environment?

In software testing, a test environment refers to a setup of software and hardware used for executing test cases. It is an isolated system that simulates the production environment where the software will be used. The test environment includes all the necessary resources, such as hardware, software, data, and network configuration, required to execute the test cases.

Test environments are set up to ensure that the testing process does not impact the production environment and to provide a controlled environment to identify and isolate defects. A test environment can be hosted on-premises or in the cloud, and it can be shared among team members working on the same project.

Q30 Explain the concept of browser automation?

Browser automation is the process of automating web browser interactions, such as clicking buttons, filling out forms, and navigating to different pages. This is typically done using a tool like Selenium, which allows you to write scripts in languages like Python or JavaScript that simulate user interactions in a web browser. Browser automation is commonly used in web testing to automate repetitive tasks and ensure consistent results.

Q31 Explain cross-browser testing?

Cross-browser testing refers to the process of testing a website or web application across multiple web browsers, such as Google Chrome, Mozilla Firefox, Apple Safari, Microsoft Edge, and others. Cross-browser testing aims to ensure that the website or web application performs consistently and displays correctly on different browsers and their various versions. This is important because each browser has its own rendering engine and may interpret web code differently, leading to inconsistencies in functionality and appearance.

Q32 Could you describe the objective of performing cross-browser testing?

The objective of cross-browser testing is to ensure that a website or application functions correctly and looks consistent across different web browsers and operating systems. Since different browsers interpret HTML, CSS, and JavaScript code differently, a website or application that looks and functions correctly in one browser may not work as intended in another. Cross-browser testing helps to identify and fix these issues, ensuring a better user experience for all users, regardless of the browser they are using.

Q33 Do you believe that automated testing is replacing manual testing?

In my opinion, automated tests are not replacing manual tests, but rather complement them. While automated tests can provide many benefits, such as faster and more reliable test execution, they cannot replace the human insight and creativity that manual testing can provide.

Manual testing is also necessary for exploring and testing new or complex scenarios that may not be easily automated. Additionally, manual testing can help identify usability and accessibility issues that may not be caught by automated tests.

In conclusion, while automated tests are becoming more prevalent and are a valuable addition to any testing strategy, manual testing will continue to play an important role in ensuring the quality and success of software products.

Q34 Can Protractor be considered a good option for automation testing?

Yes, Protractor is a popular open-source automation testing tool specifically designed for AngularJS and Angular applications. It is built on top of the WebDriverJS library and provides additional features such as synchronization with Angular, easy configuration, and built-in support for testing Angular-specific elements such as directives and services.

Protractor also supports various testing frameworks such as Jasmine and Mocha and integrates well with tools such as Selenium and Appium for cross-browser and mobile testing. Overall, Protractor is a powerful tool for testing Angular applications and is widely used in the industry.

Q35 Could you provide some recommendations for alternatives to Selenium for automated testing?

There are several alternatives to Selenium for web application automation testing. Some popular ones include:

1. **Cypress:** a JavaScript-based end-to-end testing framework that offers fast, reliable, and easy-to-use testing for anything that runs in a browser.
2. **TestCafe:** an open-source web automation tool that allows you to write tests in JavaScript or TypeScript, and run them on multiple browsers and platforms.
3. **Puppeteer:** a Node.js library for controlling headless Chrome or Chromium browsers, providing a high-level API to control Chrome or Chromium over the DevTools protocol.
4. **Appium:** an open-source tool for automating native, mobile web, and hybrid applications on iOS and Android platforms.
5. **Katalon Studio:** an all-in-one test automation solution that supports web, API, mobile, and desktop applications.

These are just a few examples of alternatives to Selenium, and the choice of tool depends on your specific testing requirements and project needs.

Q36 What is Robot framework and its architecture?

The Robot Framework is a generic test automation framework that uses keyword-driven testing. It provides a simple and clear syntax for creating test cases, with an easy-to-use tabular format for both test case data and keywords. The architecture is modular and extensible, with a set of core libraries and tools for web testing, database testing, and more. The framework can be extended with custom libraries written in Python or Java.

Q37 Explain CAPTCHA?

CAPTCHA stands for "Completely Automated Public Turing test to tell Computers and Humans Apart." It is a security measure designed to differentiate between humans and machines. CAPTCHAs typically involve presenting the user with an image containing distorted or obscured text, which the user must then enter correctly to prove they are a human and not an automated script or bot. This helps prevent automated attacks and spam on websites.

Q38 How to perform automate Captcha testing?

Automating CAPTCHA testing can be difficult since the purpose of CAPTCHA is to prevent automation. However, there are some techniques such as using Optical Character Recognition (OCR) tools, machine learning algorithms, and third-party services that can solve CAPTCHAs. These methods require integrating with CAPTCHA-solving APIs, which can be costly, and may not always be accurate.

Q39 Explain the working of framework?

A framework is a set of guidelines, standards, and best practices for organizing and executing software testing. It provides a structure for test automation, making it easier to develop and maintain automated tests.

Typically, a framework consists of a set of modules or components that work together to support automation testing, including test scripts, libraries, reporting tools, and other utilities. The framework provides an abstraction layer that allows testers to write test cases in a simpler, more concise format, which can be executed across multiple platforms and environments.

Q40 Can you describe the factors affecting the outcome of Automation testing?

Several factors can affect the outcome of automation testing, including:

1. **Test tool selection:** Choosing the right automation testing tool is critical for success. Each tool has its features, capabilities, and limitations. Selecting a tool that meets the requirements of the project can improve the efficiency of testing.

2. **Test script design:** Test script design is essential in automation testing. Well-designed test scripts can detect defects more efficiently and can reduce the maintenance effort required.

3. **Test data:** Test data is used to verify whether the application under test meets the required specifications. The quality of test data is crucial for the success of automation testing. Inaccurate or incomplete test data can lead to false positives or negatives.

4. **Test environment:** The test environment should be similar to the production environment to produce reliable results. Any differences between the two environments could lead to false positives or negatives.

5. **Test maintenance:** Maintaining test cases is important in automation testing. Changes in the application can affect the tests, and maintaining the test cases can ensure that the tests are updated to reflect the changes in the application.

6. **Skill level of automation engineers:** The skill level of automation engineers can affect the quality of automated tests. Experienced automation engineers can create better test scripts that are more efficient, reliable, and maintainable.

7. **Integration with other tools:** Automation testing is not done in isolation. It often involves the integration of different tools, such as defect tracking tools, continuous integration tools, and test management tools. The integration of these tools can affect the outcome of automation testing.

By taking into consideration these factors, automation testing can be a successful and efficient method of ensuring software quality.

Q41 What is the recommended scripting standard to follow when conducting automation testing?

When performing automation testing, it is essential to follow a scripting standard to ensure that the test scripts are consistent and maintainable. Several scripting standards can be followed, such as the Page Object Model (POM) or the Screenplay Pattern. POM is a popular standard that helps in creating an object repository of web pages and test scripts to interact with the elements on the page.

The Screenplay pattern is a more user-focused approach, which separates the user actions from the technical implementation of the tests. Ultimately, the chosen standard should be aligned with the project requirements and goals to achieve a successful automation testing outcome.

Q42 Describe sikuli

Sikuli is an open-source tool used for automating GUI testing. It is a visual automation tool that uses screenshots of the user interface elements as references for automation. Sikuli provides a simple and intuitive scripting language, making it easy to write and maintain test scripts. It supports both Windows and Mac operating systems and can automate desktop and web-based applications.

Sikuli also provides a feature for image recognition, which allows it to locate and interact with GUI elements even when their position on the screen changes. Overall, Sikuli is a powerful and flexible tool for GUI automation testing.

Q43 What are the differences between Sikuli and Selenium?

Sikuli is an image-based automation tool that uses computer vision to interact with graphical user interfaces, while Selenium is a web-based automation tool that controls browsers to test web applications. While both tools are used for automation testing, they differ in their approach and the types of applications they are best suited for.

Q44 Explain QTP?

QTP (QuickTest Professional), now known as UFT (Unified Functional Testing), is a test automation tool developed by HP (Hewlett-Packard) for functional and regression testing. It uses a graphical user interface to record and playback tests and supports a wide range of scripting languages, including VBScript, JavaScript, and Python. It can be used for testing web, desktop, and mobile applications, and includes a range of features for test management and reporting.

Q45 Can you provide examples of how automation testing is being used in modern applications?

Some examples of modern applications of automation testing:

1. **E-commerce websites:** Automation testing is commonly used to test the functionality and usability of e-commerce websites, such as adding items to a cart, checkout processes, and payment gateways.
2. **Mobile applications:** Automation testing is widely used to test mobile applications, including iOS and Android apps, to ensure that they work smoothly across multiple devices and platforms.
3. **Banking and finance:** Automation testing is used to test banking and financial applications, including online banking systems and trading platforms, to ensure that they are secure, reliable, and compliant with

industry regulations.

4. **Healthcare:** Automation testing is used to test electronic health records (EHR) and other healthcare applications to ensure that they are accurate, secure, and comply with regulations.

5. **Gaming:** Automation testing is used to test games, including mobile and web-based games, to ensure that they are functional and provide an optimal user experience.

6. **Internet of Things (IoT):** Automation testing is used to test IoT devices and applications, such as smart homes and wearable technology, to ensure that they function correctly and integrate seamlessly with other devices and platforms.

7. **Artificial Intelligence (AI):** Automation testing is used to test AI-based applications, including chatbots and voice assistants, to ensure that they are intelligent and provide an optimal user experience.

Q46 What are the differences between open-source, vendor, and in-house tools for automated testing?

Open source, vendor, and in-house tools are three types of tools that can be used for automated testing. Open-source tools are usually free and can be downloaded and used by anyone, whereas vendor tools are commercial products that are sold by a company. In-house tools are tools that are developed by a company for their own use.

Open-source tools often have a large community of users and developers, which can be helpful for troubleshooting and support. However, they may not always be as feature-rich as vendor tools and may require more technical expertise to use.

Vendor tools are typically more expensive but offer a wider range of features and support. They may also come with dedicated customer support and training.

In-house tools are developed specifically for the needs of a particular company and can be customized to fit their specific requirements. However, they may require significant resources to develop and maintain, and may not have the same level of support as vendor tools.

Ultimately, the choice of tool will depend on the specific needs and resources of the organization, as well as factors such as cost, support, and ease of use.

Q47 Explain TestNG and its features?

TestNG is a popular testing framework for Java-based applications. It is designed to cover a wide range of testing categories, including unit, functional, and integration testing. TestNG offers a wide range of features that make it a popular choice among developers and QA professionals.

Some of the key features of TestNG include:

1. **Annotations:** TestNG makes use of annotations to define test cases and their associated parameters. This helps to make test cases more readable and easier to understand.
2. **Test suites:** TestNG allows you to group test cases into suites, which can then be run in a specific order. This is useful when testing complex applications with multiple dependencies.
3. **Test configuration:** TestNG provides a way to configure test environments, such as setting up test data, before running test cases.
4. **Parallel execution:** TestNG allows you to run test cases in parallel, which can help to speed up the testing process.
5. **Data-driven testing:** TestNG supports data-driven testing, which allows you to run the same test case multiple times with different data sets.
6. **Reporting:** TestNG provides detailed HTML reports that show the status of each test case and the overall test run.

Overall, TestNG is a powerful testing framework that offers a range of features to make automated testing easier and more efficient. Its support for annotations, test suites, and data-driven testing, as well as its reporting capabilities and support for parallel execution, make it a popular choice for Java developers and QA professionals.

V

Selenium

Selenium is an open-source automation testing tool used for web application testing. It allows testers to write test scripts in various programming languages like Java, Python, C#, and Ruby. Selenium interacts with web browsers to automate web application testing such as form submissions, clicking buttons, navigating pages, and capturing screenshots of test results. It supports various web browsers including Google Chrome, Mozilla Firefox, and Microsoft Edge. Selenium can also be integrated with other testing tools and frameworks for efficient test automation.

Chapter 5

Selenium automates browsers.What you do with that power is entirely up to you.

– SeleniumHQ.org

Q1 Define Selenium?

Selenium is a free and open-source automated testing tool that is used to automate web browsers. It allows developers and testers to write test scripts in various programming languages, such as Java, Python, and Ruby, to automate the testing of web applications.

Selenium supports multiple browsers and operating systems and provides a suite of tools for web testing, including record-and-playback functionality, element identification, and verification, and cross-browser testing. It is widely used for functional testing, regression testing, and acceptance testing of web applications.

Q2 Explain the pros and cons of using Selenium for automated testing?

Advantages of Selenium:

1. **Open-source:** Selenium is an open-source tool that allows free use and modification of the code.
2. **Multi-platform support:** Selenium supports various platforms like Windows, Mac, and Linux.
3. **Language support:** Selenium supports various programming languages like Java, C#, Python, Ruby, JavaScript, and more.
4. **Multiple browser support:** Selenium supports major web browsers like Chrome, Firefox, Safari, and Internet Explorer.
5. **Large community support:** Selenium has a large community of developers and testers who contribute to the development and improvement of the tool.

Disadvantages of Selenium:

1. **Limited support for desktop applications:** Selenium is mainly used for web-based applications, and it has limited support for desktop applications.
2. **Requires programming knowledge:** Selenium requires programming knowledge, which can be a disadvantage for non-technical users.
3. **No built-in reporting:** Selenium does not have built-in reporting capabilities, and you need to use third-party tools or plugins for reporting.
4. **Difficulty in testing graphics and images:** Selenium has difficulty in testing graphics and images, and it requires additional tools or plugins to do so.
5. **Flaky tests:** Selenium tests can be flaky due to various reasons like network issues, browser compatibility, and others, which can lead to false positives and negatives.

Q3 Explain the elements of Selenium?

Selenium is composed of several elements or components that allow for the automation of web browsers. These elements include:

1. **Selenium IDE:** A browser extension that allows for the creation and execution of Selenium scripts in an easy-to-use interface.
2. **Selenium WebDriver:** A collection of APIs that enable the creation of automated tests in a programming language such as Java, Python, or Ruby.
3. **Selenium Grid:** A tool that allows for the distribution of tests across multiple machines, enabling the testing of large-scale applications.
4. **Selenium RC (Remote Control):** An older version of Selenium that has been replaced by WebDriver but is still used in some legacy applications.

Together, these elements provide developers with a comprehensive suite of tools for web application testing and automation.

Q4 What are the challenges and limitations of using Selenium WebDriver?

While Selenium WebDriver is a powerful tool for web automation, there are several challenges and limitations that can be encountered when using it:

1. **Cross-browser compatibility:** One of the biggest challenges of Selenium is ensuring cross-browser compatibility. Websites can appear differently in different browsers, and automated tests must be able to handle these differences.
2. **Dynamic content:** Another challenge of Selenium is dealing with dynamic content. As websites are updated, elements can appear, disappear, or move around on the page. This can make it difficult to locate elements reliably and consistently.
3. **Slow execution:** Automated tests can be slower than manual testing,

particularly if the test suite is large. This can be a limitation if quick feedback is needed on changes made to the website.

4. **Maintenance overhead:** As websites change, automated tests can break if they are not updated accordingly. Maintaining the test suite can be time-consuming and expensive.

5. **No support for desktop applications:** Selenium is specifically designed for web applications, so it cannot be used for testing desktop applications.

6. **No built-in reporting:** Selenium does not come with built-in reporting capabilities, so it is up to the user to create custom reports.

7. **No built-in support for parallel testing:** While it is possible to run Selenium tests in parallel, there is no built-in support for this functionality.

8. **No support for testing mobile applications:** Selenium cannot be used to test mobile applications natively.

Q5 Can you explain the various types of locators that are supported by Selenium?

Selenium supports several types of locators to identify web elements on a webpage:

1. **ID:** A unique identifier for an element in the DOM.
2. **Name:** A name attribute of an element.
3. **Class Name:** A class attribute of an element.
4. **Tag Name:** A tag name of an element.
5. **Link Text:** The text of a link.
6. **Partial Link Text:** A part of the link text.
7. **CSS Selector:** A CSS selector expression to match an element.
8. **XPath:** An XML path expression to locate an element in the DOM.

It is recommended to use CSS selectors or XPath expressions when other locators are not suitable or reliable enough to locate elements on a webpage.

Q6 Can you provide an explanation of the various methods available in Selenium to navigate web pages, such as going back, forward, and refreshing?

In Selenium WebDriver, the following methods can be used to navigate between web pages:

1. **navigate().to()** – To open a new web page. This method accepts a string argument containing the URL of the page to be opened.
2. **navigate().forward()** – To move forward to the next page in the browser history.
3. **navigate().back()** – To move back to the previous page in the browser history.
4. **navigate().refresh()** – To refresh the current web page.

Example:

```java
import org.openqa.selenium.WebDriver;
import org.openqa.selenium.chrome.ChromeDriver;

public class NavigateExample {

public static void main(String[] args) {

System.setProperty("webdriver.chrome.driver",
"path/to/chromedriver");
WebDriver driver = new ChromeDriver();

// Navigate to a web page
driver.navigate().to("https://www.example.com");

// Move forward to the next page
driver.navigate().forward();

// Move back to the previous page
```

```
driver.navigate().back();

// Refresh the current page
driver.navigate().refresh();

// Close the browser window
driver.quit();
    }
}
```

In this example, we have used the ChromeDriver to open the browser window and navigate between web pages using the above-mentioned methods.

Q7 Can you discuss the pros and cons of using Selenium IDE?

Selenium IDE (Integrated Development Environment) is a record and playback tool used for creating automated tests without writing code. Here are some of the advantages and disadvantages of using Selenium IDE:

Advantages:

1. **Easy to use:** Selenium IDE has a simple and intuitive interface that makes it easy to record and playback test scripts.
2. **Rapid test development:** With Selenium IDE, test scripts can be developed quickly, as it requires minimal coding.
3. **Cross-browser testing:** Selenium IDE can be used to test applications across different browsers such as Chrome, Firefox, and Internet Explorer.
4. **Customizable:** Selenium IDE allows users to customize test cases with user-defined functions, loops, and conditional statements.

Disadvantages:

1. **Limited functionality:** Selenium IDE is limited in its functionality compared to other Selenium tools. It is best suited for small and simple

tests and cannot be used for complex testing scenarios.

2. **No support for programming languages:** Selenium IDE does not support programming languages such as Java, Python, or C#. This can be a significant limitation for users who prefer to write scripts in these languages.

3. **No support for dynamic elements:** Selenium IDE cannot handle dynamic elements on a webpage. As a result, tests recorded using Selenium IDE may fail when run on dynamic web applications.

4. **Limited test coverage:** Selenium IDE can only be used to test web applications, limiting its test coverage to only web applications.

Q8 In what situations is it appropriate to use Selenium IDE?

Selenium IDE is a good choice when creating simple automated tests, especially for those who have limited programming knowledge. It can be used for creating quick prototypes, exploring website functionalities, and performing quick regression tests. However, it has limited capabilities for complex testing scenarios and cannot be used for testing on multiple browsers or devices.

Q9 Which OS does Selenium supports?

Selenium supports multiple operating systems including Windows, macOS, Linux, and Unix-like operating systems. This is because Selenium is a cross-platform testing framework that is designed to support testing on different environments and browsers. Therefore, it can be used to test web applications on any platform that supports popular web browsers like Chrome, Firefox, Safari, and Edge.

Q10 Explain synchronization?

Synchronization, in the context of software testing, refers to the process of making sure that the test scripts execute consistently and reliably, regardless of the underlying performance of the system or network.

This is achieved by inserting appropriate wait mechanisms and timing strategies into the test script so that the script waits for the application or webpage to load or respond before executing the next action or assertion. The goal is to prevent errors and failures caused by race conditions, timing issues, or other synchronization problems that may occur during test execution.

Q11 What are the techniques used to achieve synchronization in WebDriver?

Synchronization in WebDriver refers to the techniques used to manage timing issues between the test automation script and the application under test. In Selenium WebDriver, synchronization can be achieved through the use of implicit waits, explicit waits, and fluent waits.

- **Implicit waits:** Set a global wait time that applies to all elements in the script, providing a default wait time for the entire execution of the test case.
- **Explicit waits:** Wait for a specific condition to be met before proceeding to the next step of the test script. These waits are applied to specific elements.
- **Fluent waits:** Combine implicit and explicit waits, and allow the test script to wait for a specific condition to be met before proceeding to the next step of the script. Fluent waits provide greater flexibility by allowing users to configure the polling frequency, timeout duration, and the condition that needs to be met before continuing with the test script.

Q12 Define Locator?

In Selenium, a locator is a method to identify web elements on a web page. Locators are used to locate an element on a web page to perform an action or retrieve data from it.

Q13 How might you recover specific properties from CSS to Selenium?

In Selenium, the **getCssValue()** method can be used to retrieve the value of a certain CSS property. The method takes a string parameter that specifies the CSS property name and returns the property value as a string. For example, to retrieve the font size of an element, the following code can be used:

```
WebElement element = driver.findElement(By.id("myElement"));
String fontSize = element.getCssValue("font-size");
```

Similarly, other CSS properties like color, background-color, width, height, etc. can also be retrieved using the **getCssValue()** method.

Q14 Explain the types of XPATH?

There are two types of XPath:

1. **Absolute XPath:** The XPath expression that starts with the root node or a complete path from the root element to the desired element. It starts with a single forward slash (/) and traverses down the document tree until it reaches the desired element.
2. **Relative XPath:** The XPath expression that starts with the double forward slash (//) and selects elements from anywhere in the document, not just from the root node. It is used to select elements based on their position relative to other elements or based on their attributes.

Q15 What is Absolute path?

In XPath, an absolute path refers to the complete path from the root element to the target element in the XML document. It starts with a single forward slash (/) which represents the root node and then goes on to specify each successive node until the target element is reached.

It is called an absolute path because it starts from the top of the document and gives the exact location of the element, regardless of its context. An example of an absolute path is /html/body/div[1]/p[2]/a, which specifies the second link element (a) nested inside the second paragraph (p) of the first div element in the HTML body.

Q16 What is Relative path?

In XPath, a relative path is a path that starts from the current node or a given node and navigates through the nodes in the XML hierarchy to reach the desired element. It is a path that does not start with the root node, but with a specific node in the XML structure.

Relative paths are often shorter and more flexible than absolute paths since they can be adjusted more easily when the XML structure changes. Relative paths are represented using a combination of node names, attribute names, and XPath functions, separated by forward slashes (/).

Q17 Explain the purpose of the driver.get("URL") and driver.navigate().to("URL") commands and highlight their differences?

Both **driver.get("URL")** and **driver.navigate().to("URL")** commands are used to navigate to a specified URL in Selenium WebDriver. However, there are some differences between the two.

driver.get("URL") command loads the specified URL in the current browser window or tab. If there is any ongoing page loading, it stops and loads the new URL. This method waits for the page to load completely before proceeding with the next steps.

driver.navigate().to("URL") command is used to navigate to the specified URL, but it provides some additional features like backward and forward navigation. It maintains the browser history so you can use the browser's back and forward buttons to navigate to the previously loaded pages.

Another difference is that **driver.navigate().to("URL")** is an instance method of the **WebDriver.Navigation** class, whereas **driver.get("URL")** is a convenience method of the WebDriver class.

In summary, both commands can be used to navigate to a specified URL, but **driver.navigate().to("URL")** provides additional navigation features, while **driver.get("URL")** is a simple and straightforward way to load a new URL.

Q18 Can you provide examples of expected conditions that can be used in Explicit waits in Selenium?

Expected Conditions in Selenium are used in Explicit Waits to determine if a certain condition has been met before proceeding with the next step in the test. Some of the commonly used Expected Conditions are:

1. **titleContains()** – checks if the page title contains a certain text
2. **visibilityOf()** – checks if an element is visible on the page
3. **elementToBeClickable()** – checks if an element is clickable
4. **textToBePresentInElement()** – checks if a certain text is present in a given element
5. **stalenessOf()** – checks if an element is no longer present in the DOM
6. **presenceOfElementLocated()** – checks if an element is present on the page
7. **frameToBeAvailableAndSwitchToIt()** – checks if a frame is available and switches to it
8. **alertIsPresent()** – checks if an alert is present on the page.

These conditions can be used with the WebDriverWait class to wait for a specific time until the condition is met before proceeding to the next step in the test.

Q19 Can you list some common exceptions that are encountered while using Selenium?

There are several commonly encountered exceptions in Selenium, including:

1. **ElementNotVisibleException:** This exception occurs when an element is not visible on the page, so it cannot be interacted with.
2. **NoSuchElementException:** This exception occurs when an element cannot be found on the page, typically because the locator used to find the element is incorrect.
3. **TimeoutException:** This exception occurs when a command takes longer

to execute than the amount of time specified in an explicit wait.

4. **StaleElementReferenceException:** This exception occurs when a previously referenced element no longer exists in the DOM, typically because the page has been refreshed or modified in some way.

5. **ElementNotSelectableException:** This exception occurs when an element is present on the page but cannot be selected, typically because it is disabled or read-only.

6. **WebDriverException:** This is a catch-all exception that can occur for a variety of reasons, including network connectivity issues, browser crashes, or unexpected errors within the Selenium code itself.

Q20 Explain Page Object Model or POM?

Page Object Model (POM) is a design pattern used for designing automation testing frameworks for web applications. It is used to create an object repository for web elements on a web page and also to define methods that operate on those elements.

In the POM design pattern, each web page in the application is represented as a separate class, and the web elements and actions that can be performed on those elements are defined within that class. This makes the code more modular, maintainable, and reusable. The POM design pattern can also help reduce code duplication and improve code readability.

Q21 Explain the advantages of POM?

The advantages of Page Object Model (POM) in Selenium WebDriver are:

1. **Better code maintainability:** Since the page objects are kept separate from the test code, any changes in the application UI can be easily accommodated in the page objects without affecting the test code.

2. **Reusability:** The page objects can be reused across multiple tests, reducing the amount of code duplication and making it easier to maintain.

3. **Improved readability:** POM provides a clear separation of concerns between the test code and the page objects, making the code more readable and easier to understand.

4. **Reduced test script creation time:** With POM, the creation of test scripts becomes faster as most of the work is already done in the page objects.

5. **Enhanced test script reliability:** Since POM provides a structured approach to web application testing, the chances of error in the test scripts are significantly reduced.

Q22 Write data in excel file using selenium?

To write data into an Excel file using Selenium WebDriver, we need to use a third-party library such as Apache POI.

Example code to write data to an Excel file:

```java
import java.io.FileOutputStream;
import org.apache.poi.ss.usermodel.Cell;
import org.apache.poi.ss.usermodel.Row;
import org.apache.poi.xssf.usermodel.XSSFSheet;
import org.apache.poi.xssf.usermodel.XSSFWorkbook;

public class WriteExcelFile {
public static void main(String[] args) throws Exception {
// Create a workbook instance
XSSFWorkbook workbook = new XSSFWorkbook();

// Create a sheet object
XSSFSheet sheet = workbook.createSheet("Sheet1");

// Create a row object
Row row = sheet.createRow(0);

// Create a cell object
Cell cell = row.createCell(0);

// Set cell value
```

```java
cell.setCellValue("Hello, World!");

// Write the workbook to a file
FileOutputStream outputStream = new FileOutputStream("data.xlsx");
workbook.write(outputStream);
workbook.close();
}
}
```

In this example, we create a workbook, sheet, row, and cell objects using the Apache POI library. We then set the cell value and write the workbook to a file using a FileOutputStream object. This code will create an Excel file named "data.xlsx" with the text "Hello, World!" in cell A1.

Q23 Read data in excel file using selenium?

To read data from an Excel file in Java using Selenium WebDriver, you can use the Apache POI library. Here is an example of how to read data from an Excel file:

1) Add the Apache POI dependency to your project. You can add the following dependency to your Maven project:

```xml
<dependency>
  <groupId>org.apache.poi</groupId>
  <artifactId>poi</artifactId>
  <version>4.1.2</version>
</dependency>
```

2) Create an instance of the File class with the path to your Excel file.

```java
File file = new File("path/to/your/excel/file.xlsx");
```

3) Create an instance of the FileInputStream class with the File object.

```
FileInputStream inputStream = new FileInputStream(file);
```

4) Create an instance of the XSSFWorkbook class with the FileInputStream object.

```
XSSFWorkbook workbook = new XSSFWorkbook(inputStream);
```

5) Get the sheet you want to read from using the getSheet() method of the XSSFWorkbook class.

```
XSSFSheet sheet = workbook.getSheet("Sheet1");
```

6) Iterate over the rows in the sheet using a for loop and get the cell values using the getRow() and getCell() methods of the XSSFSheet class.

```
for (int i = 0; i <= sheet.getLastRowNum(); i++) {
XSSFRow row = sheet.getRow(i);
String value1 = row.getCell(0).getStringCellValue();
double value2 = row.getCell(1).getNumericCellValue();
System.out.println("Value 1: " + value1);
System.out.println("Value 2: " + value2);
}
```

7) Close the FileInputStream and the workbook.

```
inputStream.close();
workbook.close();
```

This is just an example and you can modify it to fit your needs. Also, don't forget to handle any exceptions that may occur when reading the Excel file.

Q24 What is Headless browser testing? Explain Headless testing pros and cons?

Headless browser testing is a way of running browser tests without actually displaying the browser GUI. The browser runs in the background and executes the tests, but the user does not see any actual browser window or graphical user interface.

Advantages of headless browser testing include:

- **Faster execution:** Running tests without a GUI can save time and resources, as there is no need to render and display the UI.
- **Scalability:** Headless browser testing can be easily scaled to run multiple tests in parallel, making it suitable for large and complex test suites.
- **Platform independence:** Since the tests run in the background, they can be executed on any platform or operating system.

Disadvantages of headless browser testing include:

- **Debugging issues:** Debugging issues can be difficult, as there is no UI to observe the tests running or to interact with the browser during execution.
- **Limited support:** Some older or less commonly used browsers may not have support for headless mode.
- **Missing certain user interaction:** Some tests may require user interaction, such as clicking on certain UI elements, which is not possible in headless mode.

Q25 How to do Database testing in Selenium?

Selenium is primarily a web testing tool and is not designed for database testing. However, it is possible to perform database testing using Selenium by integrating it with a database testing framework such as DbUnit or JDBC.

General steps to achieve database testing in Selenium:

1. Connect to the database using a JDBC driver and establish a connection to the database.
2. Write SQL queries to fetch data from the database.
3. Execute the queries using the JDBC connection.
4. Validate the data returned by the query with the expected values.
5. Report the test results.

One way to achieve this is to create a separate utility class in Java that is responsible for connecting to the database, executing queries, and returning results. This class can be called from the Selenium test code to fetch the required data and validate it against the expected values.

Note that database testing is a complex process and requires a good understanding of SQL queries and database schema. It is recommended to use a dedicated database testing framework to simplify the process and ensure reliable results.

Q26 Explain JavaScriptExecutor and how JavaScriptExecutor will help in Selenium automation?

JavaScriptExecutor is an interface provided by Selenium WebDriver to execute JavaScript code using WebDriver instance. It allows you to execute JavaScript code from within your Selenium WebDriver script to manipulate the web page in ways that are not possible with Selenium WebDriver API.

You can use JavaScriptExecutor in Selenium WebDriver in cases where WebDriver API is not capable enough to perform certain actions. For example, to perform actions like scrolling a web page, highlighting a web element, or handling browser pop-ups.

JavaScriptExecutor can also help you in handling AJAX calls on the web page by waiting for the AJAX call to complete before proceeding with the test execution. This can be achieved by using the "waitForAjaxComplete" method, which polls the document.readyState property until it becomes "complete" and there are no pending AJAX requests.

Overall, JavaScriptExecutor is a powerful tool that can help you extend the capabilities of Selenium WebDriver and make your test automation scripts more robust and reliable.

Q27 How does Selenium WebDriver handle Ajax calls?

Ajax calls are asynchronous requests made by web pages to retrieve data without requiring a page reload. Handling Ajax calls is important in Selenium WebDriver because it can cause synchronization issues when automating tests.

One way to handle Ajax calls in Selenium WebDriver is to use Explicit Waits. Explicit Waits allow the test to wait for a specific condition to occur before proceeding. In the case of Ajax calls, we can wait for a specific element to appear on the page or for the Ajax loader to disappear.

Another way to handle Ajax calls is to use JavaScriptExecutor. By using JavaScriptExecutor, we can execute JavaScript commands in the context of the current page. For example, we can execute a JavaScript command to check if an element is present or not.

In addition, Selenium provides a built-in method called "waitForAjax" to handle Ajax calls. This method waits for all the Ajax requests to be completed before moving on to the next step in the test.

Overall, handling Ajax calls is crucial to ensure that the test automation runs smoothly and accurately.

Q28 List different mouse actions that can be performed?

In Selenium WebDriver, the following mouse actions can be performed using the Actions class:

1. **click()** - Clicks on the current mouse location
2. **doubleClick()** - Double clicks on the current mouse location
3. **contextClick()** - Right clicks on the current mouse location
4. **moveToElement(WebElement element)** - Moves the mouse to the center of the specified web element
5. **dragAndDrop(WebElement source, WebElement target)** - Drags the source element and drops it on the target element
6. **dragAndDropBy(WebElement source, int xOffset, int yOffset)** - Drags the source element and drops it at the given offset from the current position of the mouse
7. **release()** - Releases the current mouse button

These actions can be used to perform complex interactions with web elements, such as drag and drop, hover, and right-click actions.

Q29 Differentiate between setSpeed() and sleep() methods?

In Selenium WebDriver, both setSpeed() and sleep() methods are used for adding wait time, but they work differently.

- **setSpeed() method**: It adds a delay between two Selenium WebDriver API calls. It is used to simulate slow user actions and slow down the execution speed of test scripts.
- **sleep() method:** It pauses the execution of the script for a specified time in milliseconds. It does not distinguish between Selenium WebDriver API calls and does not wait for any event to complete.

Therefore, setSpeed() method is used for simulating slow user actions and for making the test execution slow, while sleep() method is used for adding a static delay to the script execution. It is recommended to use explicit waits and expected conditions instead of the sleep() method for synchronizing with the web elements.

Q30 Explain Page Factory?

Page Factory is a design pattern used in Selenium WebDriver to create an object repository for web elements on a web page. It is an extension of the Page Object Model design pattern and provides a mechanism to initialize web elements using the @FindBy annotation.

By using Page Factory, the initialization of web elements is done in a centralized way, making the code cleaner and more maintainable. It also provides a way to implement lazy loading, which reduces the start-up time of the test suite. Overall, Page Factory helps in creating a more robust and scalable test framework.

Q31 How should a dropdown be handled in Selenium WebDriver? How can I choose a value from the dropdown?

To handle a dropdown in Selenium WebDriver, we need to use the Select class provided by Selenium. The Select class provides different methods to interact with the dropdown. Here are the steps to handle a dropdown using Selenium WebDriver:

1. Identify the dropdown element using locators such as ID, Name, XPath, or CSS Selector.
2. Create an object of the Select class and pass the dropdown element as a parameter to its constructor.
3. Use the different methods provided by the Select class to interact with the dropdown.

Example code to select a value from a dropdown:

```java
// Import the necessary packages
import org.openqa.selenium.By;
import org.openqa.selenium.WebDriver;
import org.openqa.selenium.WebElement;
import org.openqa.selenium.support.ui.Select;

// Identify the dropdown element
WebElement dropdownElement = driver.findElement(By.id("dropdown"));

// Create an object of the Select class
Select dropdown = new Select(dropdownElement);

// Select the option by value
dropdown.selectByValue("value");

// Select the option by index
```

```
dropdown.selectByIndex(2);

// Select the option by visible text
dropdown.selectByVisibleText("Option 3");
```

In this example, we first identified the dropdown element using its ID. Then, we created an object of the Select class and passed the dropdown element as a parameter to its constructor. Finally, we used the selectByValue(), selectByIndex(), and selectByVisibleText() methods to select the desired option from the dropdown based on its value, index, or visible text.

Q32 How to Use Selenium to create Web Elements?

In Selenium, web elements can be created using the WebElement interface. The WebElement interface represents an HTML element on a webpage and provides methods to interact with it.

To create a web element in Selenium, first, we need to locate it using any of the locators such as ID, name, class name, CSS selector, or XPath. Once we have located the element, we can create an instance of the WebElement interface as follows:

```
WebElement element = driver.findElement(By.("locator value"));
```

Here, **driver** is the instance of the WebDriver, and **<locator strategy>** can be any of the supported locator strategies such as id, name, class name, css selector, or xpath. **<locator value>** is the value of the locator strategy.

After creating the WebElement instance, we can use its methods to interact with the element. For example, we can click on the element using the click() method, get its text using the getText() method, set its value using the sendKeys() method, and so on.

Q33 How can we get attributes?

To get attributes using WebDriver, we can use the getAttribute() method on the WebElement. We need to pass the attribute name as a parameter to this method to retrieve its value.

Q34 How can we get TagName?

In Selenium WebDriver, you can get the tag name of an element using the getTagName() method of the WebElement interface. This method returns the tag name of the element as a string.

Q35 How to put a value in an Alert?

To send a value into an alert, first, switch to the alert using the command **driver.switch_to.alert()**. Then, use the **send_keys()** method to send the value and **accept()** to accept the alert.

For example:

```
alert = driver.switch_to.alert
alert.send_keys('value')
alert.accept()
```

Q36 How Does Selenium Handle Web-Based Alerts/Pop-Ups?

To handle web-based alerts/pop-ups in Selenium, you can use the Alert interface provided by WebDriver. You can use the switchTo() method to switch to the alert and then use the accept(), dismiss(), or getText() methods to handle the alert.

For example,

To accept an alert:

```
// Switch to the alert
Alert alert = driver.switchTo().alert();


// Click on the OK button
alert.accept();
```

To dismiss an alert:

```
// Switch to the alert
Alert alert = driver.switchTo().alert();


// Click on the Cancel button
alert.dismiss();
```

To get the text of an alert:

```
// Switch to the alert
Alert alert = driver.switchTo().alert();


// Get the text of the alert
String alertText = alert.getText();
```

Q37 In Selenium, How Do You Handle Window-Based Alerts/Pop-Ups?

Window-based alerts/pop-ups are also known as native pop-ups. To handle these types of pop-ups in Selenium, we need to use the Alert interface provided by WebDriver.

Here are the steps to handle window-based alerts/pop-ups in Selenium:

1. Switch to the alert using the switchTo() method:
2. Alert alert = driver.switchTo().alert();
3. Get the text from the alert using the getText() method:

4. String alertText = alert.getText();
5. Accept or dismiss the alert using the accept() or dismiss() method respectively:
6. alert.accept(); // to accept the alert
7. alert.dismiss(); // to dismiss the alert
8. Enter text into the alert (if it is a prompt alert) using the sendKeys() method:
9. alert.sendKeys("Text to enter");
10. Switch back to the default content using the defaultContent() method:
11. driver.switchTo().defaultContent();

Note: It is important to switch back to the default content after handling the alert, otherwise subsequent operations may fail.

Q38 In Selenium, how do you handle multiple popup windows??

To handle multiple popup windows in Selenium, you can follow these steps:

1. Create a Set object to store the window handles.
2. Get the handle of the current window and add it to the set.
3. Click the link/button that opens the popup window.
4. Switch to the new window using the getWindowHandles() method and select the new handle.
5. Perform the necessary actions on the popup window.
6. Close the popup window using the close() method.
7. Switch back to the main window using the getWindowHandles() method and select the original handle.

Q39 How can I tell if an element will be chosen or not?

To know if an element will be selected or not, you can use the isSelected() method in Selenium WebDriver. This method returns a boolean value that indicates whether or not the element is selected. You can then use an assertion or conditional statement to check the value and perform further actions based on the result.

Q40 In Selenium, how can we switch from one frame to another frame?

To switch from one frame to another frame using Selenium WebDriver in Java, you can use the switchTo() method to switch the focus of the driver to a new frame.

Here's an example code to switch to a frame:

```
// Locate the frame element
WebElement frameElement = driver.findElement(By.id("frame-id"));

// Switch to the frame
driver.switchTo().frame(frameElement);

// Perform actions on elements inside the frame

// Switch back to the default content
driver.switchTo().defaultContent();
```

In this example, we first locate the frame element using its ID, then switch the focus of the driver to that frame using the switchTo().frame() method. After performing the necessary actions inside the frame, we switch the focus back to the default content using switchTo().defaultContent().

Q41 How to obtain the number of frames on a page?

To get the number of frames on a page in Selenium WebDriver, you can use the driver.findElements() method with the By.tagName("iframe") locator strategy to get a list of all iframe elements and then get the size of the list. This will give you the number of frames on the page.

Q42 How to fetch cell value from the table?

To get the cell value from the table in Selenium WebDriver, first, locate the table using a suitable selector, then locate the specific row and column using index or attribute, and finally use the getText() method to retrieve the text content of the cell.

For example, **driver.findElement(By.xpath("//table//tr[2]//td[3]")).get-Text()** will retrieve the text content of the 3rd column in the 2nd row of the table.

Q43 Explain the working of Radio Buttons?

To work with radio buttons in Selenium WebDriver, first, we need to identify the radio button element using the findElement() method. Then, we can use the isSelected() method to check if the radio button is already selected. To select a radio button, we can use the click() method on the radio button element.

Q44 How can I tell whether an element is enabled or not?

To know if an element is enabled or not, we can use the isEnabled() method in Selenium WebDriver. This method returns a boolean value - true if the element is enabled, and false if it is disabled. We can use this method to check the state of the element and perform actions accordingly.

For example:

```java
WebElement element = driver.findElement(By.id("myElement"));
if (element.isEnabled()) {
    // perform action on the element
} else {
    // do something else
}
```

Q45 How can I tell if a button is enabled on a page?

To check if the button is enabled on the page, you can use the isEnabled() method of the WebElement class. This method returns a boolean value indicating whether the element is enabled or not.

Here's an example code in Java:

```java
// Find the button element
WebElement button = driver.findElement(By.id("myButton"));

// Check if the button is enabled
if(button.isEnabled()) {
    System.out.println("Button is enabled");
} else {
    System.out.println("Button is disabled");
}
```

In this example, we first find the button element using its ID. Then we call the isEnabled() method on the element to check if it is enabled or not. If the button is enabled, we print a message saying so. Otherwise, we print a message saying that it is disabled.

Q46 Using AutoIt tool how to upload a file?

AutoIt is a tool that allows automating GUI testing and scripting on Windows desktop applications. It can also be used for automating file uploads in Selenium tests.

Here are the steps to upload a file using AutoIt in Selenium:

1. Download and install AutoIt from the official website.
2. Write a separate AutoIt script that selects the file to be uploaded and clicks on the "Open" button.
3. Compile the AutoIt script into an executable file.
4. Use the Runtime.getRuntime().exec() method in Java to run the AutoIt executable file from the Selenium script.
5. Wait for the file upload to complete before moving on to the next step.

Here is an example code in Java for uploading a file using AutoIt:

```java
//Click on the file upload button
WebElement uploadButton = driver.findElement(By.id("file-upload"));
uploadButton.click();

//Run the AutoIt executable file to upload the file
String autoItScript = "C:\\path\\to\\AutoIt\\script.exe";
Runtime.getRuntime().exec(autoItScript);

//Wait for the file upload to complete
WebDriverWait wait = new WebDriverWait(driver, 10);
wait.until(ExpectedConditions.invisibilityOfElementLocated
(By.id("loading-indicator")));
```

In the above example, we first locate the file upload button using the findElement() method and click on it. Then, we run the AutoIt executable file using the Runtime.getRuntime().exec() method. Finally, we wait for the file upload to complete before moving on to the next step using the WebDriverWait class.

Q47 Differentiate between driver.findElement() and driver.findElements()?

In Selenium WebDriver, driver.findElement() and driver.findElements() are two commonly used commands for locating web elements on a web page. The main differences between these two commands are:

1) **Return Type:**

- driver.findElement() returns a single web element that matches the specified locator strategy and locator value.
- driver.findElements() returns a list of web elements that match the specified locator strategy and locator value. If no elements are found, it returns an empty list.

2) **Exception Handling:**

- driver.findElement() throws NoSuchElementException when it cannot find the element on the page.
- driver.findElements() returns an empty list if the element is not found, and does not throw an exception.

3) **Usage:**

- driver.findElement() is used when interacting with a single web element on a page.
- driver.findElements() is used when interacting with multiple web elements on a page.

Example: Suppose we have a webpage with multiple input fields with the same class name 'inputField'. If we want to interact with the first input field using driver.findElement(), we can use the following code:

```
WebElement inputField =
driver.findElement(By.className("inputField"));
inputField.sendKeys("Some text");
```

If we want to interact with all input fields using driver.findElements(), we can use the following code:

```
List<WebElement> inputFields =
driver.findElements(By.className("inputField"));
for(WebElement field : inputFields) {
    field.sendKeys("Some text");
}
```

Q48 With one example, describe desired Selenium capabilities?

Desired capabilities in Selenium are a set of key-value pairs that can be used to specify the characteristics of the browser and the system under test.

Here is an example of how to use Desired capabilities in Selenium WebDriver for Chrome:

```
import org.openqa.selenium.WebDriver;
import org.openqa.selenium.chrome.ChromeDriver;
import org.openqa.selenium.remote.DesiredCapabilities;
import org.openqa.selenium.remote.RemoteWebDriver;
import java.net.URL;

public class DesiredCapabilitiesExample {

    public static void main(String[] args) throws Exception {

        // Set the desired capabilities for Chrome
        DesiredCapabilities capabilities =
        DesiredCapabilities.chrome();
```

```
capabilities.setCapability("platform", "Windows 10");
capabilities.setCapability("version", "latest");

// Create the remote WebDriver using Selenium Grid
WebDriver driver = new RemoteWebDriver(new
URL("http://localhost:4444/wd/hub"), capabilities);

// Navigate to the website
driver.get("https://www.google.com");

// Close the browser
driver.quit();
    }
  }
```

In this example, we are setting the desired capabilities for Chrome, specifying the platform as Windows 10 and the version as the latest. We then create a RemoteWebDriver using these capabilities and Selenium Grid. Finally, we navigate to the Google website and close the browser. By using Desired capabilities, we can customize the behavior of the browser and the system under test.

Q49 What does the sentence WebDriver driver = new FirefoxDriver() mean; ?

The statement WebDriver driver = new FirefoxDriver(); is used to create a new instance of FirefoxDriver, which is a class that implements the WebDriver interface.

Here, WebDriver is an interface in Selenium that provides methods to interact with a web browser. driver is a reference variable of type WebDriver that points to the new instance of the FirefoxDriver class.

When this statement is executed, a new instance of the Firefox browser is launched, and the WebDriver interface methods can be used to navigate to web pages, interact with page elements, and perform other actions on the browser.

Q50 In Selenium WebDriver, how do you send the ALT/SHIFT/CONTROL keys?

To send the ALT/SHIFT/CONTROL key in Selenium WebDriver, we can use the Actions class. Python example of how to send the ALT key:

```python
from selenium import webdriver
from selenium.webdriver.common.keys import Keys
from selenium.webdriver.common.action_chains import ActionChains

driver = webdriver.Chrome()
driver.get("https://www.example.com")

actions = ActionChains(driver)
actions.key_down(Keys.ALT)
actions.perform()
```

Similarly, to send the SHIFT key, we can use Keys.SHIFT and to send the CONTROL key, we can use Keys.CONTROL. Python example:

```python
from selenium import webdriver
from selenium.webdriver.common.keys import Keys
from selenium.webdriver.common.action_chains import ActionChains

driver = webdriver.Chrome()
driver.get("https://www.example.com")

actions = ActionChains(driver)
actions.key_down(Keys.SHIFT)
actions.perform()

actions = ActionChains(driver)
actions.key_down(Keys.CONTROL)
actions.perform()
```

Q51 Explain Selenese?

Selenese is the scripting language used by Selenium IDE to create automated tests for web applications. It is a set of commands that allow testers to interact with web pages and perform actions such as clicking buttons, filling out forms, and verifying page content.

Selenese commands are simple and easy to use, and can be recorded in Selenium IDE or written manually in a text editor. Some examples of Selenese commands include open, click, type, verifyText, and assertTitle. The use of Selenese allows for efficient and effective creation of automated tests for web applications.

Q52 List down the different types of Selenese?

There are three types of Selenese commands:

1. **Actions:** These commands are used to perform an action on a web page, such as clicking on a button, entering text into a form field, or selecting an option from a dropdown list.
2. **Accessors:** These commands are used to retrieve data from a web page, such as the value of a form field or the text of an element.
3. **Assertions:** These commands are used to verify that a certain condition is true on a web page, such as the presence of an element or the text on a page.

Selenese commands can be used to create test cases that can be run repeatedly to verify the functionality of a web application. They can also be used to create automated tests that can be integrated into a continuous integration (CI) system.

Q53 WebDriver has several benefits over Selenium RC an you explain them?

WebDriver has several benefits over Selenium RC, including:

1. **No need for a separate server:** WebDriver communicates directly with the browser using its native support for automation. In contrast, Selenium RC requires a separate server to inject JavaScript into the browser.
2. **Support for multiple browsers:** WebDriver supports multiple browsers, including Chrome, Firefox, Safari, and Internet Explorer. Selenium RC only supports Firefox and Internet Explorer.
3. **Better performance:** WebDriver uses a more efficient architecture that makes it faster and more stable than Selenium RC.
4. **More intuitive API:** WebDriver provides a more intuitive API that is easier to learn and use than Selenium RC.
5. **Supports more programming languages:** WebDriver supports a wide range of programming languages, including Java, Python, Ruby, C#, and more. Selenium RC only supports a limited set of programming languages.

Q54 What exactly is a Marionette, how does it operate, and when should it be used?

Marionette is a WebDriver implementation for Mozilla Firefox browser. It is a Gecko-based browser automation driver that allows you to control Firefox from your code, in the same way, you would control any other browser using Selenium WebDriver.

Marionette works by establishing a connection between your Selenium script and the Firefox browser. It uses the WebDriver API to communicate with the browser and enables you to execute commands and interact with elements on the page.

Marionette is useful when you need to automate testing in Firefox, as it provides a reliable and stable way to interact with the browser. It also offers some advanced features like the ability to interact with Firefox preferences, and support for advanced debugging features.

However, it should be noted that Marionette has a few limitations, such as being slower than other WebDriver implementations and having limited support for Firefox add-ons. Therefore, it is recommended to use it only when you need to test specifically in Firefox, or when you need to test features that are unique to Firefox

Q55 Explain WebDriverBackedSelenium?

WebDriverBackedSelenium is a class in Selenium that allows users to write Selenium tests using both the Selenium WebDriver API and the Selenium RC API. This means that users can leverage the benefits of both APIs in their tests.

WebDriverBackedSelenium acts as a bridge between the two APIs. It uses an instance of the Selenium WebDriver to drive the browser, and an instance of the Selenium RC API to interact with the browser using Selenium commands.

One of the main use cases for WebDriverBackedSelenium is when users have an existing Selenium RC test suite that they want to run using the WebDriver API. By using WebDriverBackedSelenium, users can gradually migrate their test suite to use the WebDriver API without having to rewrite all of their tests at once.

Q56 How to execute only failed test cases?

To run only the failed test cases in TestNG, you can use the **testng-failed.xml** file. This file is generated in the output directory by TestNG after the execution of test cases. It contains information about the failed test cases from the previous run.

To run only the failed test cases, you need to follow these steps

1) Add the below code in your testng.xml file:

```xml
<listeners>
    <listener class-name="org.testng.IReporter"></listener>
    <listener class-name="org.testng.ITestListener"></listener>
    <listener
    class-name="org.testng.IAnnotationTransformer"></listener>
    <listener
    class-name="org.testng.IExecutionListener"></listener>
    <listener class-name="org.testng.IRetryAnalyzer"></listener>
    <listener
    class-name="org.testng.TestListenerAdapter"></listener>
</listeners>
<suite name="failedSuite">
    <test name="failedTest">
        <listeners>
            <listener
            class-name="org.testng.TestListenerAdapter"></listener>
        </listeners>
        <parameter name="isRetry" value="false" />
        <classes>
            <class name="com.package.SampleTest">
                <methods>
                    <include name="testMethod1" />
                    <include name="testMethod2" />
                    <!-- Add failed methods here -->
                </methods>
            </class>
        </classes>
    </test>
</suite>
```

2) Make sure to add the testng-failed.xml file in your project's classpath.

3) Run the following command to run only the failed test cases:

```
java org.testng.TestNG testng-failed.xml
```

This will run only the failed test cases from the previous run.

Q57 How to determine Tooltip Using WebDriver?

To identify a tooltip using WebDriver in Selenium, you can use the getAttribute() method to retrieve the text of the tooltip. The steps to identify a tooltip are as follows:

1. Identify the element that has the tooltip.
2. Use the getAttribute() method to retrieve the value of the "title" attribute of the element.
3. The value of the "title" attribute is the text of the tooltip.

Here is an example code snippet to identify the tooltip using WebDriver in Java:

```
WebElement element =
driver.findElement(By.xpath("//button[@title='Click me']"));
String tooltip = element.getAttribute("title");
System.out.println("Tooltip text: " + tooltip);
```

In this example, we are identifying the button element with the "title" attribute set to "Click me". We then use the getAttribute() method to retrieve the value of the "title" attribute, which is the text of the tooltip. Finally, we print the tooltip text to the console.

Q58 Explain the types of WebDriver API available in Selenium?

There are several WebDriver API available in Selenium. Here are some of them:

1. **FirefoxDriver:** Used to automate the Firefox browser.
2. **ChromeDriver:** Used to automate the Chrome browser.
3. **SafariDriver:** Used to automate the Safari browser.
4. **InternetExplorerDriver:** Used to automate the Internet Explorer browser.
5. **EdgeDriver:** Used to automate the Microsoft Edge browser.
6. **OperaDriver:** Used to automate the Opera browser.
7. **AndroidDriver:** Used to automate the Android platform's built-in browser.
8. **IOSDriver:** Used to automate the iOS platform's built-in browser.
9. **RemoteWebDriver:** Used to connect to a remote WebDriver server, such as Selenium Grid.

Each API has its own set of methods and capabilities for interacting with the corresponding browser or platform.

Q59 How to execute multiple test suite in Selenium by using testing?

To run multiple test suites in Selenium using TestNG, follow the below steps:

1. Create a new TestNG XML file or use an existing one.
2. Add multiple test suite tags within the <suite> tag, each with a unique name attribute.
3. Within each test suite, add the <test> tag with a unique name attribute.
4. Within each test tag, add the <classes> tag to specify the classes to be included in the test.
5. Specify the test class names within the <class> tag.

6. Save the TestNG XML file and run it as a TestNG suite from the command line or an IDE.

Example TestNG XML file:

```xml
<!DOCTYPE suite SYSTEM "http://testng.org/testng-1.0.dtd">
<suite name="My Test Suite">

    <test name="Test Suite 1">
        <classes>
            <class name="com.example.TestClass1"/>
            <class name="com.example.TestClass2"/>
        </classes>
    </test>

    <test name="Test Suite 2">
        <classes>
            <class name="com.example.TestClass3"/>
            <class name="com.example.TestClass4"/>
        </classes>
    </test>

</suite>
```

In the above example, there are two test suites: "Test Suite 1" and "Test Suite 2". Each test suite contains two test classes. You can add as many test suites and test classes as needed.

Q60 Why Cross Browser Testing is necessary?

Cross Browser Testing is the process of testing a web application or website across different web browsers and platforms to ensure its compatibility with multiple devices, operating systems, and web browsers.

It is necessary because different web browsers can render the same website differently, leading to issues such as broken layouts, broken functionality, and inconsistent user experience. Cross Browser Testing helps to identify such issues and ensures that the website or application works seamlessly across different web browsers and platforms.

Q61 In addition to Maven, what are various other build and deploy tools used in the industry.?

There are several build and deploy tools apart from Maven used in the industry. Some of the popular ones are:

1. **Gradle:** It is a build automation tool used for Java projects. It provides support for building, testing, and deploying software.
2. **Jenkins:** It is an open-source automation server used for building, testing, and deploying software.
3. **Ant:** It is a Java-based build tool used for building and deploying Java projects.
4. **Bamboo:** It is a continuous integration and deployment tool used for building, testing, and deploying software.
5. **TeamCity:** It is a continuous integration and deployment tool used for building, testing, and deploying software.
6. **Travis CI:** It is a hosted continuous integration service used for building, testing, and deploying software.
7. **CircleCI:** It is a continuous integration and deployment tool used for building, testing, and deploying software.
8. **CodeShip:** It is a cloud-based continuous integration and delivery platform used for building, testing, and deploying software.
9. **GitLab CI/CD:** It is an open-source continuous integration and deployment tool used for building, testing, and deploying software.

These tools provide automation for building, testing, and deploying software, making the development and deployment process faster and more efficient.

Q62 Explain the different network protocols that Selenium supports?

Selenium supports several network protocols, including:

1. **HTTP (Hypertext Transfer Protocol):** The most commonly used protocol for web browsing.
2. **HTTPS (Hypertext Transfer Protocol Secure):** A secure version of HTTP that uses SSL/TLS encryption to protect data transmission.
3. **FTP (File Transfer Protocol):** A standard network protocol used to transfer files from one host to another over a TCP-based network, such as the Internet.
4. **SFTP (Secure File Transfer Protocol):** A secure version of FTP that uses SSH encryption to protect data transmission.
5. **SMTP (Simple Mail Transfer Protocol):** A protocol used for sending and receiving email.
6. **TCP/IP (Transmission Control Protocol/Internet Protocol):** A suite of protocols used for communication between network devices.

Selenium primarily uses HTTP and HTTPS for web communication.

Q63 Explain Continuous Integration (CI) and also tell its benefits?

Continuous Integration (CI) is a software development practice in which developers frequently integrate code changes into a shared repository. With each integration, an automated build and test process is triggered to detect issues and bugs early in the development cycle. This process allows for faster and more frequent releases, as well as greater collaboration and accountability among team members.

Benefits of CI include:

1. **Early detection of issues:** CI allows for the detection of issues and bugs

early in the development cycle, before they can become larger and more difficult to fix.

2. **Faster feedback:** CI provides immediate feedback to developers on the status of their code changes, allowing them to quickly address issues and make necessary adjustments.

3. **Improved quality:** CI ensures that each code change is thoroughly tested and integrated into the larger codebase, reducing the risk of errors and defects in the final product.

4. **Increased collaboration:** CI encourages greater collaboration among team members, as each integration is automatically shared with the rest of the team and can be quickly reviewed and tested.

5. **Greater efficiency:** CI streamlines the development process by automating the build and test process, reducing the amount of manual effort required, and allowing developers to focus on writing code.

Q64 Explain robot class?

The Robot class in Java is used to generate native system input events for test automation, self-running demos, and other applications where control over the mouse and keyboard is required.

It provides control over the mouse and keyboard devices and can be used to automate any task in the operating system, including interacting with non-browser applications. In the context of Selenium, the Robot class can be used to handle file uploads or downloads, simulate

Q65 How do you implement the Robot class in Selenium?

The Robot class in Selenium is used to perform some low-level actions on the web page such as pressing keys, clicking the mouse, etc. Here are some of the methods to implement the Robot class in Selenium:

1. Create an instance of the Robot class using the constructor.

2. Use the appropriate method to perform the action. For example, to press a key, use the keyPress method, and to release the key, use the keyRelease method.

3. If required, use the delay method to add a pause between actions.

4. After performing the actions, close the Robot instance using the dispose method.

Q66 How Database Can be accessed from Selenium?

To access a database from Selenium, we need to use external libraries that provide APIs for database connectivity. Some of the popular libraries are JDBC (Java Database Connectivity), ODBC (Open Database Connectivity), and Hibernate. We can use these libraries to establish a connection to the database, perform queries, and retrieve data.

Once we have established a connection to the database, we can use SQL commands to retrieve data and perform other operations. We can then use this data in our test cases to validate the behavior of the application.

It is important to note that database testing is not a part of Selenium's core functionality. However, Selenium can be integrated with other libraries and tools to perform database testing as a part of the overall test automation strategy.

Q67 How to discover broken links on a webpage with the Webdriver?

To find broken links on a webpage using WebDriver, we can follow these steps:

1. Navigate to the webpage whose links we want to test using the get() method of WebDriver.

2. Collect all the links on the page using findElements() method, which returns a list of WebElements.

3. Iterate through the list of links and get the value of the href attribute of each link using the getAttribute() method of WebElement.

4. Make an HTTP request to the URL obtained in step 3 using HttpURLConnection class and get the response code.

5. Check if the response code is greater than or equal to 400, which indicates a broken link.

Q68 What kinds of data have you worked with in Selenium to automate web applications?

Selenium can handle various types of data to automate web applications, such as:

1. Text input data for filling out forms or entering search queries.
2. Numeric data for calculations or performing mathematical operations.
3. Date and time data for scheduling tasks or checking time-sensitive features.
4. Checkbox and radio button data for selecting options.
5. Dropdown and multi-select box data for selecting options from a list.
6. File upload and download data for handling file input and output.
7. Alert and popup data for handling dialog boxes or confirming user actions.
8. Captcha data for handling verification codes or security features.
9. Dynamic data such as AJAX, JSON, or XML for handling real-time updates or API calls.
10. Database data for testing database connectivity, queries, and data retrieval.

Q69 How multiple screenshots can be taken in Selenium WebDriver?

To take multiple screenshots in Selenium WebDriver, you can create a loop that performs the actions for which you want to take screenshots and takes a screenshot after each action.

Here is an example code in Java:

```java
import org.openqa.selenium.WebDriver;
import org.openqa.selenium.chrome.ChromeDriver;
import org.openqa.selenium.OutputType;
import org.openqa.selenium.TakesScreenshot;
import java.io.File;
import java.io.IOException;

public class ScreenshotExample {
public static void main(String[] args) {
// Set the path of the ChromeDriver executable
System.setProperty("webdriver.chrome.driver",
"path/to/chromedriver");
// Create a new ChromeDriver instance
WebDriver driver = new ChromeDriver();
// Navigate to the webpage you want to test
driver.get("https://www.example.com");
// Loop through the actions and take a screenshot after each action
for (int i = 1; i <= 3; i++) {
// Perform an action
// ...
// Take a screenshot
File screenshotFile = ((TakesScreenshot)
driver).getScreenshotAs(OutputType.FILE);
try {
// Save the screenshot with a unique name
String screenshotName = "screenshot" + i + ".png";
File destinationFile = new File(screenshotName);
FileUtils.copyFile(screenshotFile, destinationFile);
} catch (IOException e) {
e.printStackTrace();
```

```
    }
  }
  // Close the browser
  driver.quit();
    }
  }
```

In this example, the loop runs three times, and after each iteration, it takes a screenshot and saves it with a unique name (e.g., screenshot1.png, screenshot2.png, screenshot3.png). The screenshots are saved in the same directory as the Java file. You can modify the loop to fit your specific needs.

Q70 Explain Action Class?

The Action Class in Selenium WebDriver is a way to handle advanced user interactions like mouse hover, double click, drag and drop, etc. It is used to generate complex user gestures and simulate them on the web application under test.

The Action Class consists of a series of actions or operations that need to be performed, which can be combined to perform complex operations like click-and-hold, mouse hover, etc. It can be instantiated using the Actions class in Selenium WebDriver.

Q71 How to extract text input from a text box?

You can get the typed text from a text box using the getAttribute() method in Selenium WebDriver. This method retrieves the value of the specified attribute of the web element. In the case of a text box, the getAttribute("value") method can be used to retrieve the typed text.

Python example:

```python
from selenium import webdriver

driver = webdriver.Chrome()

# Navigate to the website
driver.get("http://www.example.com")

# Find the text box and enter text
text_box = driver.find_element_by_name("text")
text_box.send_keys("Hello, World!")

# Get the typed text from the text box
typed_text = text_box.get_attribute("value")
print(typed_text)

# Close the browser window
driver.quit()
```

In this example, the send_keys() method is used to enter text into the text box. Then, the get_attribute() method with the parameter "value" is used to retrieve the typed text, which is stored in the typed_text variable. Finally, the typed text is printed to the console.

Q72 What is the process to clear the text entered in a text box?

To clear the contents of a text box in Selenium WebDriver, we can use the clear() method. The clear() method is used to clear the text from an editable text field.

Example of how to use the clear() method to clear the contents of a text box in Java:

```java
WebElement textBox = driver.findElement(By.id("textbox"));
textBox.clear();
```

In this example, we first locate the text box using findElement() method and the By.id locator strategy. Then, we use the clear() method to clear the contents of the text box.

Q73 Explain Implicit wait?

Implicit wait is a type of wait in Selenium WebDriver that sets a default waiting time for the web elements to appear on the page. It is a global wait that is applied throughout the script and is set only once per session.

When implicit wait is used, the WebDriver instance will wait for a specified amount of time for the web element to be present before throwing a NoSuchEle mentException. If the element is found before the specified time, the script will continue its execution immediately without waiting for the remaining time.

The implicit wait can be set using the driver.manage().timeouts().implicitly-Wait() method and the wait time is specified in seconds

Q74 Explain explicit wait?

Explicit wait is a technique in Selenium WebDriver that allows the script to wait for a certain condition to occur before proceeding with the execution of the next step. It is a more precise way of waiting compared to implicit wait, as it only waits for a particular element to meet a specific condition before moving on.

Explicit wait can be used with different conditions, such as the element to be clickable, visible, or to have a certain text or attribute value. The explicit wait can be implemented using the WebDriverWait class in Selenium WebDriver.

Q75 Explain Fluent Wait and also explain its use in WebDriver?

Fluent Wait is a type of Explicit Wait in Selenium WebDriver that allows a tester to define the maximum amount of time to wait for a certain condition to be met, as well as the frequency with which to check for the condition. It offers a more flexible and customized way of waiting for elements as compared to the other types of explicit waits in Selenium.

To use Fluent Wait in WebDriver, we need to first create an instance of the Wait class, passing the WebDriver instance and the maximum wait time as arguments. Then, we can chain various conditions using the until() method until the expected condition is met.

Python example of how to use Fluent Wait to wait for an element to be clickable

```python
from selenium.webdriver.common.by import By
from selenium.webdriver.support.ui import WebDriverWait
from selenium.webdriver.support import expected_conditions as EC
from selenium.webdriver.common.keys import Keys
from selenium.webdriver.support.ui import Select
from selenium.webdriver.common.action_chains import ActionChains
from selenium.webdriver.common.alert import Alert
from selenium.webdriver.common.desired_capabilities import
DesiredCapabilities
from selenium import webdriver

driver = webdriver.Chrome()

wait = WebDriverWait(driver, 10)

element = wait.until(EC.element_to_be_clickable((By.ID,
'element_id')))
element.click()

driver.quit()
```

In this example, we first import the necessary classes from the Selenium library. Then, we create an instance of the Chrome WebDriver. We create a new instance of the Wait class, passing in the WebDriver instance and the maximum wait time of 10 seconds. We then use the until() method to wait for the element with the ID "element_id" to be clickable. Once the element is clickable, we use the click() method to click on it. Finally, we quit the WebDriver instance.

Q76 Explain ElementNotVisibleException?

ElementNotVisibleException is a type of exception that is thrown when an element is present in the DOM (Document Object Model) but is not visible on the web page. This means that the element is either hidden by CSS or JavaScript or is not in the current view of the web page.

This exception is often encountered while automating web applications using Selenium WebDriver, and it indicates that the element cannot be interacted with because it is not visible to the user.

Q77 Explain Desired capabilities?

Desired Capabilities is a way to communicate with the Selenium WebDriver about the properties and settings of the browser that you want to execute your tests on. It is a key-value pair where the key represents the setting you want to apply and the value represents the value of that setting.

Desired Capabilities can be used to set the browser name, browser version, operating system, screen resolution, proxy settings, and other browser-specific properties. They are passed as an argument to the WebDriver instance to initialize the browser session with the desired settings.

Q78 How can the Login button be clicked using an alternative method?

One alternate way to click on the Login button is by using the submit() method of the form element. Assuming that the Login button is inside a form element, we can locate the form element and call its submit() method to perform the click action.

Example Python code:

```python
from selenium import webdriver

# create webdriver instance
driver = webdriver.Chrome()

# navigate to the login page
driver.get("https://example.com/login")

# enter username and password
username = driver.find_element_by_id("username")
username.send_keys("myusername")
password = driver.find_element_by_id("password")
password.send_keys("mypassword")

# locate the login form and submit it
login_form = driver.find_element_by_id("login-form")
login_form.submit()
```

In this example, we first navigate to the login page and enter the username and password. Then we locate the login form using its id attribute and call its submit() method to click on the Login button.

Q79 Can you explain how to perform a right-click action using WebDriver?

To perform right-click using WebDriver, we can make use of the Actions class.
Example code:

```
// Create an instance of the Actions class
Actions actions = new Actions(driver);

// Locate the element on which we want to perform right-click
WebElement element = driver.findElement(By.id("element-id"));

// Right-click on the element using contextClick() method of the
Actions class
actions.contextClick(element).perform();
```

In the above code, we first create an instance of the Actions class. Then, we locate the element on which we want to perform right-click using any of the locators. Finally, we use the contextClick() method of the Actions class to perform right-click on the element, and perform() method to execute the action.

Q80 What is the process to perform a drag and drop operation using WebDriver?

To perform drag and drop using WebDriver, we need to use the Actions class. The Actions class provides a method named dragAndDrop() which can be used to drag and drop elements.
For example:

```
WebElement source = driver.findElement(By.id("source"));
WebElement target = driver.findElement(By.id("target"));

Actions actions = new Actions(driver);
actions.dragAndDrop(source, target).build().perform();
```

In this example, we first locate the source and target elements using the findElement() method. We then create an instance of the Actions class and call the dragAndDrop() method, passing in the source and target elements as arguments. Finally, we call the build() method to create the action and the perform() method to perform the action.

Note that there are also other methods provided by the Actions class for performing drag and drop, such as dragAndDropBy(), which allows you to drag an element by a certain offset.

Q81 Can you provide instructions for uploading a file using WebDriver?

To upload a file using Selenium WebDriver, we can follow the below steps:

1. Identify the 'input' tag which is used to upload a file.
2. Use the 'sendKeys' method to set the file path in the input tag.

Example code snippet in Java:

```
//Locate the file input element using the 'id' attribute
WebElement fileInput = driver.findElement(By.id("fileInput"));

//Set the file path to the file input element using 'sendKeys'
method
fileInput.sendKeys("path/to/file");
```

Note that the path to the file should be absolute or relative to the current working directory of the program.

Q82 Explain same-origin policy?

The same-origin policy is a security feature implemented in web browsers that restricts a web page from accessing or interacting with resources from a different origin. The origin of a web page is defined as the protocol, domain, and port number. The same-origin policy prevents malicious scripts from hijacking user sessions and accessing sensitive information.

In Selenium, the same-origin policy can cause issues while trying to automate tests on web pages with content from different domains. To handle this issue, we can use browser options to disable the same-origin policy. For example, in Chrome, we can launch the browser with the **- -disable-web-security** option. However, this can make the browser vulnerable to security risks, and it is not recommended to use in production environments.

Another approach is to use a proxy server to redirect requests to the same domain. This can be achieved using browser plugins like Proxy Auto-Config (PAC). In PAC, we can specify rules to redirect requests to the same domain or block requests to other domains. This approach is more secure, but it requires additional setup and maintenance.

Q83 Explain the different types of navigation commands?

In Selenium, there are three types of navigation commands:

1. **get()** – It is used to load a new webpage in the current browser window. It accepts a string parameter as the URL of the webpage to be loaded.
2. **navigate().to()** – It is used to load a new webpage in the current browser window. It also accepts a string parameter as the URL of the webpage to be loaded.
3. **navigate().back()** and **navigate().forward()** – These commands are used to navigate back and forth in the browser history. **navigate().back()** loads the previous URL in the browser history, while **navigate().forward()**

loads the next URL in the browser history.

Q84 Is it possible to debug tests in Selenium IDE and if so, how can it be done?

Yes, it is possible to debug tests in Selenium IDE. Here are the steps:

1. First, make sure the Selenium IDE is open and the test script that needs to be debugged is loaded.
2. Click on the "Run" button to start the test.
3. Once the test starts running, pause the execution at the point where you want to start debugging by clicking on the "Pause" button.
4. After pausing the execution, you can use the "Step" and "Run" buttons to execute the test one step at a time or execute the test until the next breakpoint is encountered.
5. You can also use the "Debugging" tab to view the execution stack, breakpoints, and watch expressions.
6. Once you have finished debugging, you can resume the test execution by clicking on the "Resume" button.

In summary, the Selenium IDE provides a built-in debugger that can be used to step through test scripts and troubleshoot issues.

Q85 What is the Object Repository in Selenium and how can it be created?

In Selenium, an object repository is a centralized place where web elements and their locators are stored for easy maintenance and accessibility. It allows for a clear separation between test code and object details.

There are two ways to create an object repository in Selenium:

1. **Using properties file:** The web element and its locator details are stored in a separate properties file in this method. The test code can read these

properties from the file and use them for automation.

2. **Using Page Factory:** The Page Factory is a class provided by Selenium that is used to initialize web elements using the @FindBy annotation. The @FindBy annotation uses locators such as id, name, class name, etc. to locate web elements on a web page. These elements can be used in the test code by initializing the Page Factory and calling the elements by their respective names.

Q86 In Selenium, how to take a screenshot?

In Selenium, taking a screenshot can be done using the TakesScreenshot interface. Here's how to take a screenshot in Selenium WebDriver:

```
// Create a WebDriver instance
WebDriver driver = new ChromeDriver();

// Navigate to the webpage
driver.get("https://example.com");

// Take a screenshot and store it in a file
File screenshot = ((TakesScreenshot)
driver).getScreenshotAs(OutputType.FILE);

// Save the screenshot to a file
FileUtils.copyFile(screenshot, new File("screenshot.png"));
```

VI

JUnit

JUnit is a popular open-source testing framework for Java-based applications. It provides a set of annotations, assertions, and test runners that help developers write and run unit tests. JUnit supports different types of tests such as parameterized tests, exception tests, and test suites. It also integrates with build tools like Maven and Gradle to automate test execution as part of the software development lifecycle. JUnit has been widely adopted as a standard for unit testing in the Java community and is known for its ease of use and extensibility.

Chapter 6

JUnit is a simple framework to write repeatable tests. It is an instance of the xUnit architecture for unit testing frameworks.

– Kent Beck

Q1 Why is JUnit important?

JUnit is important in software testing as it is a unit-testing framework for the Java programming language. JUnit makes it easy to write and run repeatable tests, which is essential for ensuring that code changes do not introduce new bugs. The framework provides several assertions and annotations for developers to use, which simplifies the testing process and ensures that tests are comprehensive.

Additionally, JUnit can be integrated with build systems like Maven and Gradle, which makes it easy to automate the testing process and include it as part of a continuous integration and delivery pipeline.

Q2 How to use JUnit?

JUnit is a testing framework used for writing and running unit tests for Java applications. To use JUnit, you need to first add the JUnit library to your project's classpath. Then, you can write test methods with annotations such as @Test, which will be executed by JUnit when you run the test class. You can also use assertions and other JUnit features to verify the behavior of your code.

Q3 Can you provide some recommended techniques for using JUnit effectively?

Here are some best practices for using JUnit:

1. **Write clear and concise test cases:** Test cases should be easy to read and understand, with clear inputs and expected outputs.
2. **Use annotations properly:** JUnit provides several annotations such as @Test, @Before, @After, and @Ignore. Use them appropriately to ensure proper test case execution and reporting.
3. **Create reusable test code:** Avoid duplicating test code by creating reusable methods and classes.
4. **Organize test cases:** Group related test cases together to make it easier to maintain and execute them.
5. **Use parameterized tests:** Parameterized tests allow you to execute the same test case with different sets of input data.
6. **Use assert methods effectively:** Use the assert methods provided by JUnit to validate the output of your test cases.
7. **Keep test cases independent:** Each test case should be independent of others, so that a failure in one test case does not affect the execution of other test cases.
8. **Use code coverage tools:** Use code coverage tools such as JaCoCo to ensure that your tests are covering all the code paths in your application.
9. **Use a continuous integration (CI) server:** Use a CI server such as Jenkins or Travis CI to automatically build and run your tests every time code is committed to the repository.
10. **Continuously review and refactor test code:** Regularly review and refactor your test code to ensure that it remains maintainable and efficient.

Q4 What are some of the difficulties or obstacles that one may encounter while using JUnit?

Some challenges that can be associated with using JUnit:

1. **Lack of User Interface:** JUnit is a command-line tool, and it lacks a user interface. This can make it difficult to visualize test results and diagnose issues that arise during test execution.
2. **Difficulty with Testing Asynchronous Code:** JUnit doesn't have native support for testing asynchronous code, which can be a challenge when testing applications that rely heavily on asynchronous processes.
3. **Time-Consuming Setup and Tear-down Processes:** Creating test data and setting up the testing environment can be time-consuming, especially if the test data needs to be created from scratch for each test run.
4. **Maintenance Overhead:** If tests are not maintained regularly, they can become outdated and no longer useful. It is important to keep tests up-to-date and relevant to the current codebase.
5. **Difficulty in Testing GUI Applications:** Testing GUI applications can be challenging with JUnit, as it doesn't provide any direct support for GUI testing.
6. **Lack of Flexibility:** JUnit is a unit-testing framework and is designed to test individual units of code. It may not be flexible enough to test more complex scenarios or integration testing.

It's important to note that these challenges can be mitigated by following best practices and utilizing other tools and frameworks in conjunction with JUnit

Q5 Should every logic have a corresponding test case?

Ideally, every logical branch of the code should have at least one corresponding test case. However, in practice, it may not be feasible to test every single line of code or every possible scenario. Test cases should be prioritized based on the level of risk and impact they can have on the software. The goal is to achieve maximum test coverage with minimum effort and resources.

Q6 Can you suggest some JUnit extensions that could be helpful in testing?

JUnit provides several extensions that can be used to add additional features or functionality to the framework. Some of the most useful JUnit extensions are:

1. **Mockito:** This extension provides the ability to create and use mock objects in JUnit tests, allowing you to test code that has dependencies on other objects or services.
2. **Parameterized:** This extension allows you to run the same test case multiple times with different input values, making it easier to test different scenarios and edge cases.
3. **Assertions:** This extension provides additional assertion methods that can be used in JUnit tests, making it easier to write tests that are more expressive and concise.
4. **JUnit Vintage:** This extension allows you to run JUnit 3 tests in JUnit 4, allowing you to migrate legacy code to the newer framework.
5. **JUnit Jupiter:** This is the latest version of JUnit, which provides new features such as nested tests, dynamic tests, and test interfaces, among others.

Q7 What happens if you set the JUnit method's return type to'string'?

JUnit methods should have a return type of void. If a JUnit method is declared with a return type of string, it will compile without errors, but it will be ignored during test execution. JUnit will only execute methods with a return type of void.

Q8 Explain XMLUnit?

XMLUnit is a Java-based open-source framework used for unit testing XML documents. It offers the ability to compare XML documents in a variety of ways, including comparing the actual and expected output of an XML document. XMLUnit provides a set of assert methods for performing XML assertions and it supports different types of XML inputs such as String, File, InputSource, DOM Nodes, and SAX InputSources.

Q9 Provide a test case for @Test annotation?

Here is an example of a test case using the @Test annotation in JUnit:

```
import org.junit.Test;
import static org.junit.Assert.assertEquals;

public class MyTest {

@Test
public void testAddition() {
int result = 1 + 1;
assertEquals(2, result);
}
}
```

In this example, the @Test annotation is used to mark the testAddition() method as a test case. The assertEquals() method is used to check if the result of the addition operation is equal to the expected value of 2. If the test passes, it means that the addition operation is working correctly.

Q10 Can you list some important JUnit annotations?

JUnit provides several annotations that can be used to define test methods, test classes, and other behaviors. Some of the significant JUnit annotations are:

1. **@Test:** It is used to mark a method as a test method.
2. **@Before:** It is used to annotate a method that should be run before each test method in the class.
3. **@After:** It is used to annotate a method that should be run after each test method in the class.
4. **@BeforeClass:** It is used to annotate a method that should be run once before all the test methods in the class.
5. **@AfterClass:** It is used to annotate a method that should be run once after all the test methods in the class.
6. **@Ignore:** It is used to annotate a test method or a test class that should be ignored during the test execution.
7. **@RunWith:** It is used to specify a custom test runner for running the tests.

These annotations help in organizing and controlling the flow of test execution and provide additional information about the tests.

Q11 Explain JUnit fixture?

In JUnit, a fixture refers to the fixed state of the test environment used for unit testing. It is created by defining a set of preconditions that are required for the test to run successfully, such as defining the inputs and expected outputs for the test method. The fixture ensures that the tests are repeatable and predictable by setting up the required conditions for each test case. The @Before and @After annotations are used to create and teardown the fixtures respectively.

Q12 Explain mocking and stubbing?

Mocking and stubbing are techniques used in testing to simulate or replace parts of the system that the unit under test depends on.

Mocking is a technique used to create a fake object that simulates the behavior of a real object in a controlled way. Mock objects are used to replace the real dependencies of the unit under test, and their behavior is predefined by the tester. Mocking is often used when the dependencies of the unit under test are too complex or time-consuming to set up in a test environment.

Stubbing is a technique used to create a simplified implementation of an object or interface that returns a fixed value when called. Stubs are used to replace parts of the system that are not relevant to the test and are often used to simulate a response from a remote system or database. Stubbing can be used to provide a simplified implementation of a complex dependency or to simulate different scenarios and edge cases in testing.

Q13 How can JUnit help with test isolation?

JUnit provides a test runner that executes test cases and provides test reports. JUnit helps in achieving test isolation by creating a new instance of the test class for each test method execution. This ensures that there are no dependencies between test methods, and each test method is executed in isolation.

JUnit also provides the @Before, @After, @BeforeClass, and @AfterClass annotations that allow developers to specify setup and teardown methods for test cases. These annotations help in maintaining the test environment and provide test isolation by resetting the state of the test environment before each test method execution.

Q14 What significance do the annotations @RunWith have?

The @RunWith annotation is used to specify the test runner to be used to execute the tests in a JUnit test class. It allows you to customize the test execution process and add additional functionality to your tests.

The default test runner in JUnit is JUnitCore, which is used to execute tests in the JUnit framework. However, you can use other test runners such as SpringJUnit4ClassRunner, Parameterized, or Suite to customize the test execution process. The @RunWith annotation is typically used in conjunction with other JUnit annotations such as @Test, @Before, @After, and @Ignore to create robust and flexible test cases.

Q15 What exactly are JUnit Assert Methods?

JUnit Assert methods are used to verify the actual result of a test against the expected result. Here are some commonly used JUnit Assert methods:

1. **assertEquals()** – This method checks that two values are equal. It takes two parameters, the expected value and the actual value.
2. **assertTrue()** – This method checks that a condition is true. It takes a boolean value as a parameter.
3. **assertFalse()** – This method checks that a condition is false. It takes a boolean value as a parameter.
4. **assertNull()** – This method checks that a value is null. It takes one parameter, the value being checked.
5. **assertNotNull()** – This method checks that a value is not null. It takes one parameter, the value being checked.
6. **assertSame()** – This method checks that two objects refer to the same object. It takes two parameters, the expected object, and the actual object.
7. **assertNotSame()** – This method checks that two objects do not refer to the same object. It takes two parameters, the expected object, and the

actual object.

8. **fail()** – This method fails a test with the specified message. It takes a message as a parameter.

Q16 Explain important features of JUnit?

JUnit is a popular testing framework in Java that offers several features to assist in writing and running unit tests. Some of the important features of JUnit include:

1. **Annotations:** JUnit provides several annotations that can be used to specify how to run a test case, which method to run before and after a test case, which method to ignore, etc.
2. **Test runners:** JUnit provides a set of test runners that can be used to execute test cases, such as the JUnitCore test runner, which can be used to execute tests from the command line.
3. **Assertions:** JUnit provides a set of assertion methods that can be used to verify the behavior of a unit of code, such as assertEquals(), assertTrue(), assertFalse(), assertNull(), assertNotNull(), etc.
4. **Test fixtures:** JUnit provides a way to create and destroy objects that are used by multiple test cases, such as the @BeforeClass, @AfterClass, @Before, and @After annotations.
5. **Test suites:** JUnit provides a way to group test cases into a suite and execute them together using the Suite runner.
6. **Parameterized tests:** JUnit allows test methods to be executed with different sets of arguments using the @Parameterized annotation.
7. **Exception handling:** JUnit provides a way to test if a method throws a specific exception using the @Test(expected=) annotation.

Q17 Explain test runner?

In JUnit, a test runner is a framework component that controls the execution of test cases and generates test results. It is responsible for running test cases, collecting and displaying test results, and generating reports. JUnit provides a built-in test runner called the JUnitCore class, which executes test cases and provides detailed information on the results.

The test runner also facilitates the use of different JUnit annotations and enables users to specify various testing configurations, such as selecting which test cases to run or the order in which they should run.

Q18 What is the purpose of the org.junit.JUnitCore class?

The org.junit.JUnitCore class provides a command-line tool to run JUnit tests. Its objective is to run JUnit test cases outside of any IDE. It provides the runClasses() method to run one or more test classes, and it can generate detailed test reports in various formats, including XML, HTML, and plain text.

Q19 What do you know about Parameterized tests?

Parameterized tests are a way to run the same test logic multiple times with different data inputs. They allow a developer to write a single test method and run it multiple times with different sets of input parameters, rather than writing multiple test methods to test the same behavior with different inputs.

This can make tests more efficient and easier to maintain. In JUnit, parameterized tests are implemented using the @Parameterized and @ValueSource annotations.

Q20 When does JUnit tests garbage collected?

In JUnit, tests are garbage collected when the test run has been completed. The test objects are created and executed during the test run, and once the test run completes, the objects are no longer needed and can be garbage collected.

This happens automatically by the Java Virtual Machine (JVM) garbage collector. However, it is important to ensure that any external resources used by the tests are properly cleaned up to avoid leaking resources.

Q21 Explain Cactus?

Cactus is an open-source framework for unit testing server-side Java code such as Servlets, JSPs, and EJBs. It provides an in-container testing mechanism that allows developers to test their server-side code as if it were being executed in a real production environment. This framework simplifies the task of testing complex distributed applications by providing a simple and easy-to-use interface for testing server-side code.

Q22 Explain the fundamental components of Cactus?

Cactus is a testing framework for Java-based server-side applications. The fundamental components of Cactus are:

1. **Test cases:** These are the classes containing test methods.
2. **Test cases decorators:** These are classes that extend the abstract class TestDecorator and can be used to add pre- and post-test functionality to the test cases.
3. **Test controllers:** These are classes that extend the abstract class ServletTestController and are responsible for the setup and teardown of the test environment.
4. **Test runners:** These are classes that extend the abstract class TestRunner and are used to execute the test cases.

5. **Ant tasks:** These are a set of Ant tasks provided by Cactus for running tests in the build process.

Q23 How does XMLUnit make use of support classes?

XMLUnit is a Java library that provides various APIs for comparing XML documents. It uses several supporting classes to perform comparison operations. Some of the important supporting classes used by XMLUnit are:

1. **Diff:** It is used to calculate the differences between two XML documents.
2. **DetailedDiff:** It is a subclass of Diff that provides a more detailed description of the differences between two XML documents.
3. **Validator:** It is used to validate an XML document against a DTD or XSD schema.
4. **XPathEngine:** It is used to evaluate XPath expressions on an XML document.
5. **Transform:** It is used to transform an XML document using XSLT.

By using these supporting classes, XMLUnit simplifies the process of comparing XML documents and makes it easier to write test cases for XML-based applications.

Q24 Explain Mock Object?

A mock object is a simulated or fake object that mimics the behavior of a real object in a controlled way. It is used to replace dependencies in a system under test (SUT) that cannot be easily instantiated or used in a test environment.

The mock object simulates the behavior of the real object, allowing for isolated testing of the SUT. Mock objects can be created manually or with the help of a mocking framework. They provide a way to test the SUT in a more controlled and predictable manner.

Q25 How to setup a JUnit test case?

To set up a JUnit test case, follow these steps:

1. **Import the JUnit framework:** Start by importing the JUnit framework into your Java program.
2. **Create a test class:** Create a new Java class for your test cases. This class should have a name that reflects the name of the class you are testing, but with "Test" appended to the end.
3. **Add test methods:** Add one or more test methods to your test class. Each test method should test a specific feature or behavior of the class you are testing.
4. **Use annotations:** Use the annotations provided by JUnit to identify which methods are test methods, and to provide setup and teardown methods that will be run before and after each test method.
5. **Write test code:** Write the code for your test methods, using the JUnit assertions to check that the code being tested is behaving correctly.
6. **Run the test:** Finally, run your test case using the JUnit test runner, either from within your IDE or from the command line. The test runner will execute all of the test methods in your test case and report the results.

Q26 Explain how JUnit can be used to test for concurrency issues?

JUnit provides several mechanisms to test for concurrency issues:

1. Using the @Test(timeout) annotation to specify the maximum amount of time a test case is allowed to run. This is useful to detect deadlocks or infinite loops in concurrent code.
2. Using the Thread class to create and manage threads in a test case. This allows you to simulate concurrent access to shared resources and test for thread safety.
3. Using the CountDownLatch class to coordinate multiple threads in a test

case. This is useful to simulate scenarios where a certain number of threads need to complete before other threads can proceed.

4. Using the ConcurrentHashMap class to test for thread safety of collections. This class provides a thread-safe implementation of the Map interface and can be used to test concurrent access to shared data structures.

5. Using the ExecutorService class to execute tasks in a pool of threads. This allows you to test scenarios where multiple tasks are executed concurrently and need to coordinate their actions.

Q27 How mock objects can be used in JUnit?

JUnit can be used to mock objects by utilizing various mocking frameworks such as Mockito or EasyMock. These frameworks provide annotations and methods to create mock objects and stub their behavior for testing purposes. The @Mock annotation can be used to create a mock object, and when and thenReturn methods can be used to stub the behavior of the mock object. The mocked object can then be used in the test case to verify the behavior of the code being tested. For example:

```
@RunWith(MockitoJUnitRunner.class)
public class MyTestClass {

@Mock
private MyObject myObject;

@Test
public void myTest() {
when(myObject.someMethod()).thenReturn("expectedResult");
// test the code using the mocked object
}
}
```

In this example, MyObject is the object being mocked, and someMethod() is the method being stubbed to return the expected result. The mock object is created using the @Mock annotation, and the when and thenReturn methods are used to set up the stubbed behavior. The MockitoJUnitRunner class is used to run the test case and inject the mock object into the test class.

Q28 How to test private methods using JUnit?

In general, it is not recommended to test private methods because they are not part of the public interface of the class and may change without notice. However, if you really need to test a private method in JUnit, you can use Java reflection to access the method.

For example:

```java
import java.lang.reflect.Method;
import org.junit.Test;
import static org.junit.Assert.*;

public class MyClassTest {

@Test
public void testPrivateMethod() throws Exception {
MyClass obj = new MyClass();
Method method = MyClass.class.getDeclaredMethod("privateMethod",
String.class);
method.setAccessible(true);
String result = (String) method.invoke(obj, "input");
assertEquals("expected output", result);
}


}
```

In this example, we create an instance of MyClass, and then use reflection to access the private method privateMethod() and invoke it with the argument "input". We then check that the result is "expected output" using assertE-quals(). Note that we need to call setAccessible(true) on the method object to bypass the access control and make the private method callable.

Q29 Differentiate between JUnit 4 and JUnit 5?

There are several differences between JUnit 4 and JUnit 5:

1. **Annotations:** JUnit 5 introduced a new set of annotations while maintaining backward compatibility with JUnit 4 annotations. Some of the new annotations introduced in JUnit 5 include @BeforeEach, @AfterEach, @BeforeAll, and @AfterAll.
2. **Architecture:** JUnit 5 has a new architecture that consists of three main components: Jupiter, Vintage, and Platform. Jupiter provides the programming model and extension model for writing tests and extensions, Vintage provides backward compatibility with JUnit 3 and 4, and Platform provides support for running tests on different platforms.
3. **Assertions:** JUnit 5 has a new set of assertions that are more powerful and expressive than JUnit 4 assertions. JUnit 5 assertions include methods like assertAll, assertTimeout, and assertThrows.
4. **Test Discovery:** JUnit 5 introduced a new way of discovering tests using Java's ServiceLoader mechanism. This allows for more flexibility in discovering tests and makes it easier to write custom test engines.
5. **Parameterized Tests:** Parameterized tests have been improved in JUnit 5 with the introduction of the @ParameterizedTest annotation and the ability to pass parameters from sources other than CSV files.
6. **Dynamic Tests:** JUnit 5 has introduced dynamic tests that allow for generating tests at runtime. This can be useful in situations where the number of tests is not known at compile time.

Overall, JUnit 5 is more powerful, flexible, and extensible than JUnit 4, and it provides a better programming model for writing tests. However, it is not backward compatible with JUnit 4, so migrating from JUnit 4 to JUnit 5 can require some effort.

Q30 Explain @Before and @After annotations in JUnit 4?

In JUnit 4, the @Before and @After annotations are used to define methods that are executed before and after each test method in a test class, respectively.

The @Before annotated method is executed before each test method and is typically used to set up the test data or any other objects needed for the test. The @After annotated method is executed after each test method and is typically used to clean up the test data or any other objects created during the test.

These annotations help in reducing code duplication and make it easier to manage the test environment.

Q31 What exactly is Mockito? How does it help you?

Mockito is an open-source testing framework for Java that allows the creation of mock objects in automated unit tests. It allows developers to simulate the behavior of real objects and test the interactions between them. Mockito provides a simple and flexible API that helps to isolate the code under test by mocking the dependencies of the unit being tested.

This can help to speed up the testing process and simplify the code by removing the need for complex setup and teardown code. Mockito can also help to identify and fix defects earlier in the development cycle by making it easier to write automated tests. Overall, Mockito can help to improve the quality and reliability of software applications by enabling more comprehensive and effective testing.

Q32 Can JUnit be executed using the command prompt?

Yes, it is possible to run JUnit from a command prompt. You can use the java command to run the JUnit test class, which should be compiled and packaged with all the necessary dependencies. Here is an example command to run a JUnit test class named MyTest:

```
java -cp .;junit-4.XX.jar;hamcrest-core-1.XX.jar
org.junit.runner.JUnitCore MyTest
```

In this command," ." represents the current directory, **junit-4.XX.jar** and **hamcrest-core-1.XX.jar** are the JUnit and Hamcrest library files, and **org.junit.runner.JUnitCore** is the main class that runs the JUnit test. MyTest is the name of the test class. You may need to modify the command based on your specific configuration and environment.

Q33 Why Mockito does not allow mocking of static methods?

Mockito can't mock static methods because the static methods are bound to the class, rather than to the object of the class. Mockito operates by creating a proxy object for the class under test, and since static methods are associated with the class rather than an instance, it is not possible to create a proxy object for them. Therefore, Mockito is designed to mock only instance methods, making it unsuitable for mocking static methods.

Q34 Differentiate between doReturn and thenReturn?

In Mockito, thenReturn and doReturn are used to specify the return value of a mocked method. However, there is a subtle difference in the way they work.

thenReturn is a standard method used to specify the return value of a mocked method. It returns the specified value when the mocked method is called. For example:

```
when(mockedObject.someMethod()).thenReturn(someValue);
```

On the other hand, doReturn is used when we need to specify the return value of a mocked method that has void as its return type or when we want to change the default behavior of the mocked method. For example:

```
doReturn(someValue).when(mockedObject).someMethod();
```

Here, we are using doReturn to specify the return value of a void method. We can also use it to change the default behavior of the mocked method. For example, we can throw an exception when a mocked method is called by using doThrow instead of thenReturn:

```
doThrow(new RuntimeException()).when(mockedObject).someMethod();
```

In summary, we use thenReturn to specify the return value of a mocked method and doReturn to change the default behavior of the mocked method or specify the return value of a void method.

Q35 In which situations mocking can be used?

Mocking is useful in situations where you want to isolate the code you are testing from its dependencies, which may be expensive, unreliable, or simply difficult to work with. Some examples of when to use mocking include:

1. Testing code that relies on external services, such as databases or web services, that may be unavailable or slow to respond during testing.
2. Testing code that depends on complex or hard-to-configure objects, such as network connections or file systems.
3. Testing code that depends on external libraries or frameworks that are not under your control.

4. Testing code that requires specific conditions or behaviors that are difficult to reproduce in a real-world environment, such as error conditions or edge cases.

Mocking can help you to simulate the behavior of these dependencies, allowing you to test your code in a controlled, predictable environment. It can also make it easier to isolate and debug issues when they arise, as you can more easily identify the source of any problems.

Q36 Explain the best practice to test a generics class?

Testing a generics class can be done in a similar way to testing a regular class. However, there are some additional considerations to keep in mind:

1. **Test with multiple data types:** Since a generics class can work with multiple data types, it's important to test the class with different data types to ensure that it works as expected with each one.
2. **Test with null values:** It's important to test the class with null values to ensure that the class can handle them properly.
3. **Test with edge cases:** It's important to test the class with edge cases, such as the minimum and maximum values for a given data type, to ensure that it works as expected in all scenarios.
4. **Use parameterized tests:** Parameterized tests can be used to test a generics class with multiple data types, making it easier to ensure that the class works as expected with each one.
5. **Use mock objects:** Mock objects can be used to test the interactions between the generics class and other objects or systems, making it easier to isolate and test specific components of the class.

Q37 How can we test private methods?

There are different ways to test private methods:

1. **Reflection:** Using reflection, it is possible to access and invoke private methods. This approach allows you to test private methods directly, but it may make your tests fragile, as changes in the implementation details of the private method could break your tests.
2. **Test the public interface that calls the private method:** If a private method is called by a public method, then it is possible to test the behavior of the private method indirectly by testing the public method that calls it.
3. **Extract the private method to a separate class:** If the private method contains a significant amount of business logic, it may be a good idea to extract it into a separate class and test it separately.
4. **Use a testing framework that supports testing of private methods:** Some testing frameworks, like PowerMock, provide support for testing private methods. However, this approach can also make your tests fragile, as changes in the implementation details of the private method could break your tests.

Q38 How to test timeout in a Java method using JUnit?

Yes, JUnit provides a feature to test for timeouts in a Java method using the @Timeout annotation. This annotation can be applied to either a test method or to the whole test class to specify the maximum amount of time that the test method(s) should be allowed to run. If the test method(s) take longer than the specified timeout, then the test will fail. For example:

```
import org.junit.jupiter.api.Test;
import org.junit.jupiter.api.Timeout;

import java.util.concurrent.TimeUnit;
```

```
public class MyTest {

@Test
@Timeout(value = 5, unit = TimeUnit.SECONDS)
public void testWithTimeout() throws InterruptedException {
// Do some time-consuming task
Thread.sleep(6000);
}
}
```

In this example, the testWithTimeout() method will fail after 5 seconds because it takes longer than the specified timeout of 5 seconds.

Q39 Can you explain the relationship between unit testing and cyclomatic complexity?

Cyclomatic complexity is a measure of the number of independent paths through a piece of code. Unit tests can be used to measure and test each independent path of the code, and thus provide a way to ensure that the code has been thoroughly tested and is free of defects.

Q40 Exolain Hamcrest Matchers?

Hamcrest Matchers are a set of matchers that can be used with testing frameworks like JUnit to perform more flexible and readable assertions in Java tests. They provide a large collection of assertion methods that allow developers to write expressive and readable tests. Hamcrest Matchers work by matching the actual value against an expected value or condition.

Q41 Differentiate between @After, @Before, @BeforeClass and @AfterClass?

In JUnit 4, the annotations @Before and @After are used to mark methods that should be run before and after each test case, respectively. These methods can be used to set up or tear down any necessary objects or configurations for each test case.

On the other hand, @BeforeClass and @AfterClass are used to mark methods that should be run only once, before, and after all the test cases in a test class. These methods are used to set up or tear down any necessary objects or configurations that are shared by all the test cases in the class.

To summarize:

- **@Before:** run before each test case
- **@After:** run after each test case
- **@BeforeClass:** run once before all the test cases in a test class
- **@AfterClass:** run once after all the test cases in a test class

Q42 We can not debug or test using System.out.println.() why?

System.out.println() is a way to print information on the console for debugging purposes, but it does not provide any structured or formal way to test and assert the output. Additionally, it is not possible to disable or remove these statements easily in production code, which can cause performance and security issues. Therefore, testing frameworks like JUnit provide better ways to write tests, with structured asserts and reports.

Q43 How can you ignore tests in JUnit?

In JUnit, you can ignore tests using the @Ignore annotation. When you annotate a test method with @Ignore, the test is skipped when the test suite is executed. This is useful when a test is known to be failing or if a test is not yet implemented and should be skipped until it is implemented. For example:

```
@Test
@Ignore("Test to be implemented later")
public void testSomeMethod() {
// Test code
}
```

Q44 What are the distinctions between JUnit and TestNG?

JUnit and TestNG are two popular testing frameworks for Java. Here are some of the key differences between them:

1. **Execution order:** TestNG supports the execution of test cases in a defined order, while JUnit executes tests in a random order.
2. **Annotation flexibility:** TestNG offers more flexible annotations than JUnit, which allows for easier customization of test behavior.
3. **Configuration:** TestNG has more advanced configuration options than JUnit, which can be useful in complex testing scenarios.
4. **Parallel execution:** TestNG offers native support for parallel execution of test cases, while in JUnit this has to be managed through third-party tools.
5. **Data-driven testing:** TestNG provides native support for data-driven testing, while in JUnit this has to be implemented using external libraries or custom code.
6. **Reporting:** TestNG offers better reporting features than JUnit, including HTML and XML reports with detailed information about test runs.

Q45 What are the best practices for writing unit test cases,?

Some best practices for writing unit test cases:

1. **Keep tests independent:** Each unit test should be independent of the others, and the tests should not depend on the order in which they run.
2. **Test only one unit at a time:** Each test should only focus on one specific unit, and not test multiple units at the same time.
3. **Name test cases properly:** Test cases should be named properly so that it is easy to identify the tests that are passing or failing.
4. **Use setup and teardown methods:** Use setup and teardown methods to create test fixtures and clean up after the tests are done.
5. **Use assertions correctly:** Use assertions to check the expected behavior of the unit being tested, and avoid using conditional statements in tests.
6. **Test all possible input values:** Test all possible input values that the unit being tested can handle, including edge cases.
7. **Keep tests fast and reliable:** Keep the tests fast and reliable, so that they can be run frequently during development.
8. **Refactor test cases:** Refactor test cases when necessary, to make them more efficient and maintainable.
9. **Continuously review and update test cases:** Continuously review and update test cases as the code changes, to ensure that the tests remain relevant and effective.

By following these best practices, developers can ensure that their unit tests are effective and maintainable, and help them catch bugs early in the development process.

Q46 Explain @Ignore annotation and its purpose?

The @Ignore annotation is used in JUnit to ignore a test method or an entire test class. When applied to a test method, it indicates that the test method should be skipped during test execution. When applied to a test class, all the test methods within that class are skipped.

This annotation is typically used when a test method is failing or not yet implemented, or when a test method does not apply to the current state of the code being tested. It is important to note that the ignored tests will not be executed during the test run.

Q47 Explain the need for org.junit.TestSuite class?

The org.junit.TestSuite class in JUnit is used to group multiple test cases into a suite and execute them together. It allows for running multiple test classes together and also provides an easy way to run tests in a specific order.

By using a test suite, developers can create a collection of tests that can be executed together and provide an overall status for the test suite as a whole. This can be particularly useful when working on large projects with multiple test classes.

Q48 Why should I use TDD? Is there anything negative about test-driven development?

Test-driven development (TDD) is a software development approach that focuses on writing automated tests before writing the actual code. TDD has several advantages, including:

1. Helps to catch bugs early in the development cycle
2. Improves code quality and maintainability
3. Provides faster feedback on code changes

4. Ensures that the code meets the requirements and specifications

However, there are also some potential disadvantages to TDD, such as the additional time and effort required to write tests, which may result in slower development cycles. Additionally, it may be difficult to apply TDD to legacy code or code that is constantly changing. Nonetheless, the benefits of TDD generally outweigh the potential drawbacks, especially for long-term software development projects.

Q49 Please provide a couple of the Unit Testing advantages for developers that you have directly encountered?

There are a few benefits of unit testing that developers commonly report:

1. **Better code quality:** Unit tests help to identify and prevent defects earlier in the development cycle, leading to higher code quality.
2. **Faster bug detection and resolution:** Unit tests can quickly detect errors, making it easier to fix them before they become more complicated and expensive to fix.
3. **Improved code maintainability:** By ensuring that each unit of code works as intended, unit testing helps to keep the codebase clean, maintainable, and easier to modify or refactor.
4. **Increased confidence in code changes:** Unit tests provide developers with the confidence to make code changes without the fear of breaking existing functionality.
5. **Easier collaboration:** Unit tests can serve as a form of documentation, making it easier for team members to understand the codebase and collaborate effectively.

VII

API Testing

API testing is a type of software testing that focuses on testing the application programming interfaces (APIs) of a software application. It involves testing various aspects of the API, including functionality, reliability, performance, security, and more. API testing is typically performed by sending requests to the API using various methods and tools, such as Postman, and verifying the responses received. It can help ensure that the API is working as expected and can integrate seamlessly with other applications and systems.

Chapter 7

Q1 Explain API?

API stands for Application Programming Interface. It is a set of protocols, routines, and tools for building software applications. APIs specify how software components should interact, enabling two separate applications to communicate with each other. In simple terms, an API allows different software applications to interact with each other and share data or functionality without requiring the user to understand the underlying code or infrastructure.

Q2 Explain API testing?

API testing is a type of software testing that involves testing application programming interfaces (APIs) to ensure that they meet functional and performance requirements. It involves testing the API endpoints, response codes, request and response payloads, headers, and error messages to ensure that they behave as expected. API testing can be performed manually or using automated tools and is an essential part of the software development lifecycle to ensure the quality and reliability of the application.

Q3 Explain test API?

Test API can refer to two different things:

1. **Testing APIs:** APIs can be tested like any other software component, to ensure that they work correctly and meet the expected functionality and performance requirements. Testing APIs involves verifying the API's inputs, outputs, error handling, and security.
2. **Testing with APIs:** Test API can also refer to a type of API used specifically for testing, sometimes called a "test harness" or "mock API." These test APIs simulate the behavior of a real API for testing purposes, allowing developers to test their software in isolation without relying on a real API or external service. Test APIs can be particularly useful for unit testing and automated testing.

Q4 Explain REST API?

REST (Representational State Transfer) is a software architectural style used for creating web services. RESTful web services are based on HTTP protocols, and they use HTTP requests to perform CRUD (Create, Read, Update, and Delete) operations on resources. REST API is an interface that enables interaction between different software systems over HTTP. It is a web-based architecture that follows a client-server model and operates on the HTTP protocol. RESTful APIs are widely used in web and mobile applications for exchanging data between the server and client.

Q5 Explain browser API?

A browser API is a set of tools and protocols used for building software applications that interact with a web browser. These APIs provide developers with a way to interact with various aspects of the browser, such as the DOM (Document Object Model), CSS styles, cookies, history, and more.

Browser APIs are often used in conjunction with other web technologies, such as HTML, CSS, and JavaScript, to create dynamic and interactive web applications. Some examples of browser APIs include the Web Audio API, the Geolocation API, the Web Storage API, and the Canvas API.

Q6 Can API be considered software?

Yes, an API can be considered a type of software. It is a set of protocols, routines, and tools for building software applications, and it defines how software components should interact with each other. In other words, an API provides a way for software to communicate and interact with other software, making it an integral part of software development.

Q7 Explain the five principles of API testing?

The five principles of API testing are:

1. Validating the correctness of data returned by the API
2. Testing for all possible error conditions
3. Verifying the response time and performance of the API
4. Checking the security aspects of the API
5. Testing the API in different scenarios and configurations.

Q8 List some types of API testings?

Some types of API testing include:

1. **Unit testing:** Testing individual functions, methods, or classes of code in isolation.
2. Integration testing: Testing how different modules or services of the system interact with each other.
3. **Functional testing:** Testing the functionality of the API, including input validation, error handling, and response validation.

4. **Load testing:** Testing the performance of the API under high loads and concurrent users.
5. **Security testing:** Testing the security of the API, including authentication and authorization, input validation, and access control.

Q9 What are some considerations to keep in mind when performing API testing?

While performing API testing, one must keep in mind the following things:

1. Test for both positive and negative scenarios.
2. Test for different input parameters and their combinations.
3. Test for error handling and response validation.
4. Test for authentication and authorization.
5. Test for performance and scalability.
6. Security test.
7. Use tools for automation and load testing.
8. Verify the API documentation.
9. Test for backward compatibility.
10. Ensure test data and environment consistency.

Q10 Explain UI testing?

UI testing is the process of testing the graphical user interface of a software application to ensure that it is functioning correctly and meets the requirements. UI testing involves validating the appearance, usability, and functionality of the user interface.

Q11 How UI testing is different from API testing?

The main difference between UI testing and API testing is that UI testing is focused on the user interface and how users interact with the application, while API testing is focused on the underlying code and how different software components interact with each other. Additionally, UI testing is often more time-consuming and complex than API testing, as it requires the use of tools such as automation frameworks and user interface testing libraries.

Q12 What types of bugs can be discovered during API testing?

Some common types of bugs that can be found during API testing include:

1. Invalid inputs or parameters
2. Incomplete or missing functionality
3. Incorrect error or status codes
4. Security vulnerabilities, such as exposed sensitive data or unauthorized access to resources
5. Performance issues, such as slow response times or high resource usage
6. Compatibility issues with different environments or platforms
7. Issues related to data integrity or consistency.

Q13 Name the methods supported by REST API and briefly explain their function.

REST API supports several HTTP methods, including:

1. GET: retrieves a representation of a resource or a list of resources.
2. POST: creates a new resource or performs an action on a resource.
3. PUT: updates a resource or replaces it with a new one.
4. DELETE: deletes a resource.
5. PATCH: updates a resource with a set of changes.
6. HEAD: retrieves the headers of a resource, without its body.
7. OPTIONS: retrieves the allowed methods, headers, and other options for a resource.

These methods are used to interact with the resources on the server and are typically mapped to CRUD (Create, Read, Update, Delete) operations on the resources.

Q14 Explain caching in REST API?

Caching in REST API refers to the process of storing the response generated by a REST API call in the client or server cache memory to reduce the number of subsequent API calls and improve performance. When a client sends a request to a REST API endpoint that supports caching, the server checks if the requested data is available in the cache memory.

If the data is available, the server retrieves it from the cache and returns the response without making another API call. This reduces the load on the server and improves the response time of the API. However, caching can sometimes lead to stale data being served if the cache is not refreshed or invalidated properly.

Q15 Is it possible to perform hacking attempts on APIs during the testing phase?

APIs can be vulnerable to security threats, including hacking if they are not designed and tested properly. It is possible to exploit security vulnerabilities in an API during testing if the tester intentionally tries to do so.

Therefore, it is important for API testers to have a strong understanding of potential security risks and to use best practices to prevent vulnerabilities, such as implementing proper authentication, encryption, and authorization protocols. Additionally, testers can use tools and techniques such as fuzz testing and penetration testing to identify and address potential security weaknesses.

Q16 An API may be hacked while being tested; how can we test an API's security?

Testing the security of an API is an essential part of API testing. Here are some ways to test the security of an API:

1. **Authorization and authentication testing:** Test the API to ensure that it requires valid authorization and authentication credentials to access the API.
2. **Parameter and boundary testing:** Test the API with invalid and unexpected values of parameters and boundary conditions to ensure that the API is not susceptible to buffer overflow, SQL injection, and other attacks.
3. **Error handling testing:** Test the API to ensure that it provides informative error messages that do not reveal any sensitive information.
4. **SSL and TLS testing:** Test the API to ensure that it uses secure SSL and TLS protocols for data transfer.
5. **Penetration testing:** Conduct penetration testing to simulate an attack on the API to identify any vulnerabilities.
6. **Code review:** Review the code to ensure that it follows secure coding practices and does not have any security loopholes.

Overall, testing the security of an API is crucial to ensure that it is safe from unauthorized access and protects the sensitive information it handles.

Q17 What are the primary tools used for API testing, considering that it can be a challenging and time-consuming task?

There are several tools available for API testing, some of the most popular ones are:

1. **Postman** - A popular tool for API testing, it offers a user-friendly interface for creating, testing, and managing APIs.
2. **SoapUI** - Another widely used API testing tool, it supports both REST and SOAP protocols and offers advanced testing features.
3. **JMeter** - Originally designed for load testing, JMeter can also be used for API testing and supports various protocols.
4. **Swagger** - An open-source tool that allows you to design, document, and test RESTful APIs.
5. **Assertible** - A cloud-based tool for API testing, it offers automated testing and continuous monitoring features.
6. **Rest-Assured** - A Java-based library for testing RESTful APIs, it integrates well with popular testing frameworks like JUnit and TestNG.
7. **Karate** - A relatively new tool for API testing, it combines API testing, mock services, and UI automation in a single framework.

These tools help automate the API testing process, which can save time and effort while ensuring more accurate and efficient testing.

Q18 What are the advantages of API testing for business?

API testing offers several advantages for businesses, some of which are:

1. **Early detection of defects:** API testing allows defects to be caught early in the development cycle, reducing the cost and time of fixing them later.
2. **Faster time to market:** API testing enables faster time to market by

reducing the testing cycle, allowing organizations to launch products and services more quickly.

3. **Better quality assurance:** By testing the API layer, it ensures the correctness and reliability of the application, providing better quality assurance.

4. **Improved customer experience:** API testing helps in ensuring that the application is responsive, accurate, and secure, which results in an improved customer experience.

5. **Cost-effective:** API testing is generally less expensive than GUI testing as it involves less manual testing and automation can be performed easily.

6. **Greater test coverage:** With API testing, it's possible to achieve greater test coverage as it is easier to test different combinations of inputs and outputs, and simulate different scenarios.

Overall, API testing provides a reliable, scalable, and efficient approach to testing that helps organizations deliver high-quality products and services to their customers.

Q19 Can you briefly explain some major forms of API testing?

Some major forms of API testing are:

1. **Unit Testing:** It involves testing the smallest unit of code that can be individually tested. In API testing, unit testing focuses on testing individual API functions to ensure that they are working as expected.

2. **Functional Testing:** It involves testing the functionality of the API by simulating real-world scenarios. In API testing, functional testing ensures that the API is working as per the requirements and specifications.

3. **Load Testing:** It involves testing the API's behavior under varying levels of load or traffic. Load testing helps to identify bottlenecks in the system and improve its performance.

4. **Security Testing:** It involves testing the API's security features to ensure

that the API is secure from potential threats such as unauthorized access, injection attacks, and other vulnerabilities.

5. **Integration Testing:** It involves testing the interaction between different components of the system to ensure that they are working together as expected. In API testing, integration testing is done to ensure that the API is integrating well with other systems and components.

6. **Penetration Testing:** It involves testing the API's ability to withstand attacks from hackers or other malicious entities. In API testing, penetration testing is done to ensure that the API is secure and can withstand potential attacks.

Q20 Do you know about API documentation? If so, could you briefly explain it?

Yes, documentation is an important aspect of API testing. API documentation provides a detailed understanding of the API endpoints, their functionalities, and how to use them. It helps developers and testers to better understand the API and its behavior.

API documentation includes information such as API endpoints, supported parameters, data types, error codes, response formats, and examples of API calls. Good documentation ensures that API testing is more efficient and effective, as testers have a clear understanding of the expected behavior and can quickly identify any issues or discrepancies. It also helps in collaboration between developers, testers, and other stakeholders involved in the development and testing process.

Q21 Explain API automation.

API automation refers to the process of automating the testing of an API. This involves writing scripts that can simulate API requests and responses, send them to the API, and then verify that the API is behaving as expected. The automation can include functional testing, performance testing, security testing, and other types of testing to ensure the API is working correctly.

API automation can help speed up the testing process, increase test coverage, and reduce the risk of errors or bugs in the software. It is a critical part of modern software development and is often used in conjunction with other types of automation, such as UI automation or database testing.

Q22 There is often confusion between API and web services. Can you provide a brief explanation of the differences between the two?

Yes, it is a common confusion among people as both API and web services serve the same purpose, i.e., data exchange between different applications.

API is a set of protocols, routines, and tools used for building software applications, and it defines the way two different software applications interact with each other. In simpler terms, it can be thought of as a messenger that delivers a request from one application to another and returns the response.

On the other hand, a web service is a type of API that specifically uses the HTTP protocol for communication over the web. A web service can be defined as a standardized way of communicating between two applications over the network. It uses the Simple Object Access Protocol (SOAP), Representational State Transfer (REST), or XML–RPC as the messaging protocol.

In summary, API is a broader term that includes web services as a type of API, while web services are specifically a type of API that uses HTTP protocol for communication over the web.

Q23 Could you provide an explanation of status codes, along with an example?

HTTP status codes are a standard set of responses given by a web server in response to a client's request. The status codes provide information about the status of the request and response between the client and the server. Here are a few examples of HTTP status codes:

1. **200 OK:** This status code indicates that the request was successful, and the server returned the requested data. For example, when you make a request for a webpage, and the server returns the requested HTML page, the response code would be 200 OK.
2. **404 Not Found:** This status code indicates that the requested resource is not available on the server. For example, if you enter the wrong URL in your browser, the server will return a 404 Not Found error.
3. **500 Internal Server Error:** This status code indicates that there is a problem with the server, and the request cannot be completed. For example, if there is an error in the server-side code, the server may return a 500 Internal Server Error.

In summary, status codes provide information about the status of the request-response cycle between a client and a server and help to identify any issues with the communication between the two.

Q24 Explain"payload" in terms of API?

In the context of API, payload refers to the data that is sent in the request or response body. It contains information in a specific format such as JSON, XML, or plain text, that is transferred between the client and server to fulfill the API request. The payload can contain parameters, metadata, and other information that is necessary to complete the request.

For example, when making a POST request to create a new resource, the payload will typically contain the data for the new resource, such as its name, description, and other relevant details.

Q25 Can you provide some real-world examples of how APIs have been utilized in the past, and the specific ways in which they were used?

Here are some real-world examples where API has been used:

1. **Google Maps API:** Google Maps API is one of the most widely used APIs. It allows developers to integrate Google Maps functionality into their applications, making it easier for users to find locations, get directions, and view maps.
2. **Twitter API:** Twitter's API allows developers to build applications that interact with the Twitter platform. Developers can use the API to post tweets, retrieve user information, and search for tweets that match specific criteria.
3. **Facebook API:** Facebook's API allows developers to build applications that interact with the Facebook platform. Developers can use the API to retrieve user information, post updates to a user's profile, and access Facebook's social graph.
4. **OpenWeatherMap API:** The OpenWeatherMap API allows developers to access weather data for any location in the world. Developers can use the API to retrieve current weather conditions, forecast data, and historical weather data.

In all of these examples, APIs were used to allow developers to integrate functionality from one application into another, making it easier for users to access the data they need.

Q26 There are complaints about the limited options available for API testing. In your opinion, are there indeed limited options for testing APIs?

No, there are several options available to test an API. Some popular tools for API testing include Postman, SoapUI, JMeter, Rest-Assured, and Karate DSL. Additionally, programming languages like Python, Java, and JavaScript also offer libraries and frameworks for API testing. With the right tools and techniques, API testing can be a comprehensive and effective process.

Q27 Protocols play a vital role in any digital system. Could you provide an explanation of their usage in APIs?

Protocols are indeed an essential part of any digital system, including API. API uses various protocols to facilitate communication between different systems. Some common protocols used in API testing include HTTP, HTTPS, SOAP, REST, and XML-RPC. These protocols ensure secure and reliable communication between the client and server, and also help to define the structure and format of the API requests and responses.

For example, HTTP and HTTPS are widely used protocols for REST API testing, while SOAP and XML-RPC use XML as the primary data format. Overall, protocols play a crucial role in API testing, ensuring the smooth and secure transfer of data between different systems.

Q28 Despite being a time-consuming and thorough process, why is API testing still considered important, and what are its benefits?

Yes, API testing has several advantages, which is why it is an essential part of software testing. Some of the benefits of API testing are:

1. **Early detection of defects:** API testing can help in detecting defects early in the development lifecycle, which reduces the overall cost of fixing them.
2. **Faster testing:** API testing is faster than UI testing as it does not require any user interface interaction.
3. **Increased test coverage:** API testing can cover a large number of scenarios and test cases, which would be difficult to test manually.
4. **Improved quality:** API testing helps in improving the overall quality of the software by identifying issues and bugs early in the development process.
5. **Automation:** API testing can be easily automated, which reduces the time and effort required for testing.
6. **Integration:** APIs are used to integrate different software components and systems, and testing APIs ensures that these integrations are working as expected.

Overall, API testing is crucial for ensuring the quality, reliability, and performance of software systems.

Q29 Could you outline the fundamental principles that govern the design of API tests?

The basic principles involved in API test design are as follows:

1. **Test the functionality of the API:** API testing should aim to test the functionality of the API thoroughly, including both positive and negative test cases.
2. **Test the input and output values:** API testing should involve testing the input and output values of the API to ensure that they match the expected values.
3. **Test for error codes and messages:** API testing should test for error codes and messages and ensure that they are consistent across the API.
4. **Test for security:** API testing should test for security vulnerabilities, including authentication, authorization, and data protection.
5. **Test for performance:** API testing should test for the performance of the API, including response time, load testing, and stress testing.
6. **Test for scalability:** API testing should test the scalability of the API to ensure that it can handle large volumes of data and requests.
7. **Test for compatibility:** API testing should test for compatibility with different operating systems, browsers, and devices.
8. **Test for documentation:** API testing should test the API documentation to ensure that it is accurate, complete, and up-to-date.

By following these principles, API testing can be designed and executed efficiently and effectively.

Q30 There are various types of API testing, but are there any standard procedures that should be followed during API testing?

Yes, there is a procedure that needs to be followed during API testing. The basic steps involved in API testing are as follows:

1. **Understanding the API specification:** The first step in API testing is to understand the API specification and the functionality that the API provides.
2. **Test environment setup:** Setting up the test environment is critical to ensuring that the API testing process is successful. This includes installing any necessary software and setting up any required configurations.
3. **Test planning:** Once the API specification is understood and the test environment is set up, the next step is to plan the tests. Test planning involves deciding on what test cases to execute, which input values to use, and how to evaluate the results.
4. **Test execution:** This step involves executing the planned tests and recording the results.
5. **Result analysis and reporting:** After executing the tests, the results are analyzed and reported. The reports can include any issues encountered during the testing, recommendations for improvements, and areas where the API performed well.
6. **Retesting:** In case any issues were found during the testing, the developers should fix them and the tests should be re-executed to ensure that the issues have been resolved.

Following these steps can help ensure that the API testing process is successful and any issues are identified and addressed.

Q31 During API testing, what are the essential elements that you check, and how do you verify them?

Fundamental things that can be checked during API testing:

1. **Endpoint Testing:** Test if the API endpoint is working properly and returning the expected response for the given request.
2. **Data Validation:** Test if the data returned by the API is valid and in the expected format, including data type, length, and content.
3. **Error Handling:** Test if the API handles errors and exceptions properly and returns the expected error response codes and messages.
4. **Performance Testing:** Test if the API can handle a large number of requests without affecting its performance and response time.
5. **Security Testing:** Test if the API is secure and follows standard security practices to prevent unauthorized access and data breaches.
6. **Integration Testing:** Test if the API integrates properly with other components of the system, such as databases, third-party services, and applications.

To perform these tests, various tools and techniques can be used, such as API testing frameworks, REST clients, testing libraries, and automated testing tools.

Q32 Despite the numerous benefits of API testing, are there any significant challenges that can arise during the process?

No, despite the advantages, there are still some challenges faced while performing API testing. Some of the major challenges include:

1. **Lack of documentation:** Some APIs may have inadequate documentation or no documentation at all, making it challenging to understand and use the API.
2. **Changes in API:** Changes in the API can cause compatibility issues and may require changes in the existing tests.
3. **Testing with external systems:** APIs are often used to communicate between different systems, so testing requires coordination with other teams and systems.
4. **Security:** APIs can be vulnerable to hacking and unauthorized access, so testing for security is crucial.
5. **Performance testing:** APIs can be used by a large number of users, so performance testing is important to ensure that the API can handle high traffic.
6. **Integration testing:** APIs are often part of a larger system, so integration testing with other components of the system is necessary to ensure seamless functioning.

Q33 What are some of the testing methodologies that fall under the umbrella of API testing?

Some testing methods that come under API testing are:

1. Functional testing
2. Security testing
3. Performance testing
4. Load testing
5. Stress testing
6. Usability testing
7. Integration testing
8. Interoperability testing
9. Scalability testing
10. Reliability testing

Q34 What is meant by the term "POSTMAN API," which is frequently encountered in the context of APIs?

Postman is an API development tool used for testing APIs. It allows users to create, share, test, and document APIs. The tool also offers features such as automated testing, API monitoring, and collaboration between team members.

Q35 In the context of APIs, what does the term "collection" refer to?

In the context of API testing, a "collection" refers to a group of related requests or API endpoints organized together in a logical order. A collection typically includes all the endpoints needed to test a specific feature or functionality of an API.

For example, a collection for testing an e-commerce website's checkout process might include endpoints for adding items to a cart, getting shipping options, applying discounts, and processing payment. Using collections makes it easier to organize and execute API tests in a structured manner. Collections can be created and managed using various API testing tools such as Postman, Swagger, and Insomnia.

Q36 The terms "SOAP API" and "REST API" are commonly encountered by those familiar with APIs. Could you explain the difference between these two types of APIs?

SOAP (Simple Object Access Protocol) and REST (Representational State Transfer) are both web service protocols used for communication between different systems. The main difference between them is the way they handle data exchange.

SOAP is a protocol that uses XML format for data exchange and relies on a formal contract called WSDL (Web Services Description Language) to describe the message format, transport protocol, and endpoint. It requires the use of XML-based messaging formats, message-oriented middleware (MOM), and provides a set of rules to define the message structure, as well as error handling and security mechanisms.

REST, on the other hand, is a simpler, more flexible architecture that relies on standard HTTP methods like GET, POST, PUT, and DELETE to perform CRUD (Create, Read, Update, Delete) operations on resources. It can use various formats such as JSON, XML, HTML, or plain text to represent data. Unlike SOAP, REST is not bound to any particular message format or middleware, making it more lightweight and easier to implement.

In summary, SOAP is a protocol that relies on a set of standards and message formats for communication, while REST is an architecture that focuses on simplicity and flexibility, using HTTP methods for communication and various formats for data exchange.

Q37 Could you provide an explanation of what is meant by the term "caching mechanism"?

In the context of web APIs, caching is often used to improve performance and reduce network traffic by caching responses to API requests. The cached responses are stored on the client-side or server-side, depending on the implementation, and subsequent requests for the same data can be served from the cache rather than making new requests to the API.

This can significantly reduce the load on the API and improve response times for clients. However, caching can also lead to issues with stale data and data consistency, which need to be managed carefully.

Q38 In the context of APIs, what is meant by the term "API framework"?

An API framework is a set of tools, guidelines, and best practices for building, testing, and managing APIs. It provides a structured approach to designing APIs and automating various tasks associated with API development and testing.

API frameworks can help developers save time and effort by providing pre-built modules and libraries for commonly used functionalities, such as authentication, input validation, error handling, and documentation generation. Some popular API frameworks include Django REST Framework, Express.js, Ruby on Rails, Flask, and Spring Framework.

Q39 There is often confusion between the terms "library" and "framework." Could you provide a brief explanation of the terms?

In the context of software development, a library refers to a collection of pre-written code modules or functions that developers can use to simplify their work. Libraries are typically written in a particular programming language and provide specific functionality to the developers who use them. They are usually invoked by including them in the code and calling specific functions from within the library.

In contrast to a framework, a library is a more focused and smaller piece of software that provides specific functionality to the developer. It does not typically dictate an application's overall structure or flow as a framework does.

Q40 Could you explain what is meant by the term "input injection," and how it can be triggered?

Input injection is a type of security vulnerability that occurs when an attacker injects malicious input into an application or system. The input can be in the form of SQL queries, scripts, or other types of data that can be executed by the application.

To invoke input injection, an attacker typically sends specially crafted input to the application with the intent of exploiting vulnerabilities in the application's input validation or data handling mechanisms. This can lead to a range of security issues, including data theft, unauthorized access, and system compromise.

Input injection can be prevented through proper input validation and data sanitization techniques, as well as other security measures such as implementing security-focused coding practices, conducting regular security assessments, and keeping software up to date with the latest security patches.

Q41 What feature enables the usage of POSTMAN servers even when offline?

Postman provides the feature of "Offline Access" that allows users to use Postman even when they are not online. It enables users to access and use collections, environments, and other data stored in Postman even without an internet connection. Once you enable offline access in Postman, it will automatically store a copy of the collections, environments, and data locally on your device, allowing you to work offline without any interruption.

Q42 What are the practical applications of caching?

Caching is the process of storing frequently accessed data in a temporary storage location, such as a cache memory, so that it can be quickly retrieved without needing to be reloaded from the original source. The main uses of caching include:

1. **Faster access to frequently accessed data:** Caching enables faster access to frequently accessed data, as it eliminates the need to retrieve the data from its original source repeatedly.
2. **Reducing server load:** Caching helps reduce the load on the server, as it reduces the number of requests to the original source.
3. **Improving application performance:** By reducing the amount of time needed to retrieve data, caching can improve the overall performance of an application.
4. **Improving user experience:** Faster access to data can improve the user experience, as it reduces the time needed to load pages or perform other tasks.
5. **Reducing network traffic:** By reducing the amount of data that needs to be transmitted over the network, caching can help reduce network traffic and improve network performance.

Q43 When we say that an API is "stateless," what does that mean?

When we say an API is stateless, it means that the API does not store any client context between requests. Each request sent to the API server contains all the information needed for the server to understand and process the request. The server does not rely on any information from previous requests sent by the client.

This approach has several benefits, including simplifying the design of the API, improving scalability, and reducing the possibility of errors due to the server relying on incorrect information from previous requests.

Q44 Explain CRUD?

CRUD stands for Create, Read, Update, and Delete. It refers to the four basic operations that can be performed on a database or resource in a system.

- **Create:** Create a new resource or record in the database.
- **Read:** Retrieve data or records from the database.
- **Update:** Modify or update an existing resource or record in the database.
- **Delete:** Remove or delete a resource or record from the database.

CRUD operations are commonly used in web development and API design, as they provide a standard set of actions that can be performed on a resource or database.

Q45 In the context of APIs, could you provide a brief explanation of the term "resource"?

n the context of web development and APIs, a resource refers to any piece of data or functionality that can be accessed by a client through a URI (Uniform Resource Identifier). This can include anything from individual files or pages, to complex objects or collections of data.

Resources are a fundamental concept in RESTful APIs, and are typically accessed using the standard HTTP methods (GET, POST, PUT, DELETE, etc.) to perform operations on the data or functionality they represent.

Q46 What is the full form of URI, and could you provide a brief explanation of what it is?

URI stands for Uniform Resource Identifier. It is a string of characters that identifies a name or a resource on the Internet. It provides a way to locate a resource and specify the action to be performed on it.

A URI has two types: URL (Uniform Resource Locator) and URN (Uniform Resource Name). A URL specifies the location of a resource on the Internet, while a URN provides a unique name for a resource but does not specify its location.

Q47 What is AJAX, and how does it differ from REST?

AJAX stands for "Asynchronous JavaScript and XML". It is a set of web development techniques that allow web pages to update content dynamically without the need for a full page refresh.

REST, on the other hand, stands for "Representational State Transfer". It is a software architectural style that defines a set of constraints to be used for creating web services. RESTful web services use HTTP methods like GET,

POST, PUT, and DELETE to interact with resources.

While AJAX is a technique for updating content dynamically, REST is a set of constraints for creating web services that can be used to interact with resources. The two are not necessarily mutually exclusive and can be used in conjunction with one another.

Q48 Could you identify some of the primary difficulties encountered during API testing?

There are several challenges faced during API testing, including:

1. **Understanding API specifications:** It can be challenging to understand the API specifications, especially when they are poorly documented or not documented at all.
2. **Integration with other systems:** APIs are often integrated with other systems, and it can be difficult to test how they interact with each other.
3. **Security concerns:** APIs can be vulnerable to security threats such as injection attacks, and it is important to ensure that appropriate security measures are in place.
4. **Handling error messages:** Error messages can be cryptic and difficult to understand, making it challenging to identify the root cause of a problem.
5. **Data validation:** API testing involves validating data that is returned by the API, and it can be challenging to ensure that the data is accurate and consistent.
6. **Testing performance:** APIs are expected to be fast and efficient, and it is important to test their performance under varying load conditions.
7. **Maintaining test environments:** Maintaining test environments can be a challenge, especially when multiple APIs are involved, and it can be difficult to ensure that all dependencies are properly configured.

Q49 Is the statelessness of REST considered an advantage or a disadvantage?

The statelessness of REST is considered an advantage. It means that each request is independent and carries all the necessary information to complete it. This allows for better scalability, reliability, and simplicity in the design of APIs. Stateless APIs also allow for easier caching and load balancing.

However, the statelessness can sometimes be a disadvantage if the API requires the maintenance of state between multiple requests. In such cases, additional techniques, such as using tokens or sessions, need to be employed.

Q50 Could you provide an explanation of what is meant by "digest authorization"?

Digest authentication is a method of HTTP authentication that uses a hash function to authenticate a user's credentials. It is a more secure alternative to basic authentication, which sends the user's credentials in clear text.

In digest authentication, the server sends a nonce value to the client, which is used in combination with the user's password and other information to generate a hash value. The client sends this hash value along with its request to the server, which then verifies the hash value to authenticate the user.

Q51 In the context of APIs, what is meant by the term "call sequencing"?

Call sequencing refers to the order in which different API calls need to be made in order to achieve a particular outcome. In many cases, the desired outcome can only be achieved by making a series of API calls in a specific order.

Proper call sequencing is important to ensure that all necessary data is available for each API call and that the desired outcome is achieved successfully.

In API testing, call sequencing is an important consideration, particularly for complex APIs with multiple endpoints and data dependencies.

Q52 Have you encountered the term "parameter validation" in the context of APIs? If so, could you provide an explanation of what it means?

Yes, I have come across the term "parameter validation" in the context of API testing.

Parameter validation is the process of verifying that the input data passed to an API meets certain criteria and is in the expected format. This involves checking the validity, range, and type of input parameters, as well as ensuring that any required parameters are present and that any optional parameters have default values.

The purpose of parameter validation is to ensure that the API behaves as expected when receiving input data from users or other applications and to prevent unexpected behavior or security vulnerabilities caused by invalid input.

Q53 In the context of APIs, could you provide an explanation of what is meant by "schema changes"?

In the context of API testing, schema changes refer to any modifications made to the structure or format of the API response. This could include changes to the data types, field names, or even the addition or removal of fields.

Schema changes can occur as a result of updates to the API, and it is important for API testers to account for these changes and ensure that any automated tests or tools are updated accordingly to reflect the new schema. Failure to address schema changes can result in broken tests and inaccurate results.

Q54 How can you explain the similarities or differences between API testing and UI testing to someone who is not from a technical background?

API testing and UI testing are two different testing techniques that are used to validate different aspects of an application.

API testing is focused on testing the functionality of the application programming interface (API) by sending requests and analyzing responses. It involves testing the individual units of code and their integration with each other to ensure that the API meets the expected functionality, reliability, and security requirements. API testing does not involve any user interface and can be automated using various testing tools.

UI testing, on the other hand, focuses on testing the user interface of the application. It involves testing the application's interface design, user interactions, and visual elements to ensure that they meet the expected usability and accessibility requirements. UI testing typically requires a human tester to manually navigate through the application, interact with its various elements, and validate the results.

In summary, API testing and UI testing are different in terms of their focus, testing approach, and automation. While API testing is focused on testing the functionality of the application's API, UI testing is focused on testing the user interface of the application.

Q55 Which form of automation testing is the most suitable, and can it replace GUI testing?

The most suitable form of automation testing depends on the specific needs and requirements of the project. GUI testing is often necessary to ensure that the user interface and experience are working as expected. However, automated API testing is also important to ensure the functionality and reliability of the underlying systems and data exchange.

Automated API testing can complement GUI testing, but it cannot completely replace it. While API testing can verify that the application's internal functions are working correctly, GUI testing is necessary to ensure that the application as a whole is functioning properly, from the user's perspective. Therefore, a combination of both automated API testing and GUI testing is usually the best approach for comprehensive testing.

Q56 When discussing essential web services, we frequently encounter the term "SOAP"; explain "SOAP" in this context.

SOAP stands for Simple Object Access Protocol. It is a protocol used for exchanging structured information between applications over the internet. It uses XML format for encoding data and provides a messaging framework for communication between two systems.

SOAP is an older web service protocol that is based on XML and is typically used in enterprise applications. It relies heavily on a formal contract between the client and the server, known as a WSDL (Web Services Description Language) file, which specifies the details of the available methods, parameters, and data types.

Unlike REST, SOAP uses a standardized set of rules for message exchange, which includes a header and a body. It also relies on a more complex messaging structure, making it more difficult to implement and requiring more bandwidth.

Q57 What are the many services given by the SOAP protocol, and how do we use them?

SOAP (Simple Object Access Protocol) is a messaging protocol that allows for exchanging of structured and typed information between distributed systems. Some of the facilities provided by the SOAP protocol are:

1. XML-based messaging: SOAP uses XML (Extensible Markup Language) to format messages sent between systems.
2. WSDL (Web Services Description Language): SOAP uses WSDL to describe the functions provided by a web service and the format of the request and response messages.
3. Interoperability: SOAP allows for interoperability between different platforms and programming languages.
4. Security: SOAP provides several security measures like encryption, digital signatures, and authentication.
5. Reliable messaging: SOAP provides reliable messaging using acknowledgments, timeouts, and retries.

To use SOAP protocol, we need to define the WSDL document that describes the web service, the message formats, and the operations provided by the service. The client can use the WSDL document to generate the code for accessing the web service. The SOAP message is then sent over HTTP protocol using the POST method.

VIII

Postman

Postman is a popular tool used for testing and debugging APIs. It provides an easy-to-use interface for sending HTTP requests and examining responses, allowing developers to quickly test their APIs and troubleshoot issues. Postman supports various authentication methods, including OAuth 2.0 and basic authentication. It also includes features for automating tests, generating documentation, and collaborating with team members. Postman can be used across multiple platforms, including Windows, Mac, and Linux, and offers both free and paid versions with additional features.

Chapter 8

Q1 Can you explain what Postman is and how it is used?

Postman is an API development and testing tool that allows developers to design, test, and document APIs. It provides a user-friendly interface for making HTTP requests, organizing collections of requests, and testing API responses.

To use Postman, users can simply download the app and start creating requests by specifying request parameters, headers, and body. The app also provides features for automating testing, collaborating with team members, and generating API documentation.

Q2 What are the difficulties encountered when using Postman?

While working with Postman, some common challenges that may be faced are:

1. **Authentication Issues:** Postman requires proper authentication credentials to access the API, and sometimes it can be challenging to get those credentials, or the credentials may not work correctly.
2. **Environment Setup:** Setting up the environment variables in Postman can be challenging, especially when dealing with complex APIs.

3. **Test Case Creation:** Creating test cases in Postman requires a good understanding of the API, and sometimes it can be challenging to create test cases for complex APIs.

4. **Performance Testing:** Performance testing using Postman requires a lot of knowledge of the API and the testing process, and it can be challenging to set up and execute the tests correctly.

5. **Version Control:** Managing version control in Postman can be challenging, especially when dealing with multiple team members working on the same API.

Q3 Can you describe effective techniques for categorizing and grouping items in Postman?

In Postman, there are two efficient approaches to classify and group things:

1. **Collections:** Collections are a way to group requests and other assets like scripts, environments, and documentation into logical containers. They can be used to organize APIs by project, client, or any other criteria that make sense for the application. You can create multiple collections and keep them organized by using folders and subfolders.

2. **Environments:** Environments are a set of key-value pairs that represent the variables needed for the API requests to work. They can be used to manage different environments like production, staging, and development. By setting up different environment variables, you can easily switch between different environments without having to update the requests manually.

Q4 Can you explain what Postman load testing tool is?

Postman provides a load-testing tool that allows users to simulate and test the performance of their APIs. With this tool, users can generate virtual users to send requests to the API, and then monitor the performance and response time of the API under different levels of load.

The tool supports different types of load testing such as ramp-up, steady state, and ramp-down. Users can also customize the requests and set up pre and post scripts for the tests. The results of the load tests can be viewed in a dashboard, which includes metrics such as response time, error rate, and throughput, among others.

Q5 What are some typical applications of load testing tools?

Load testing tools are used to simulate heavy loads on software, websites, or APIs to determine their performance and limitations. Some common uses of load testing tools are:

1. To determine the maximum number of users a website or software can handle simultaneously without crashing or slowing down.
2. To identify the bottlenecks and weaknesses in the system under a heavy load.
3. To check the scalability of the software or website by gradually increasing the load and measuring its performance.
4. To optimize the system by identifying and fixing performance issues.
5. To ensure that the system can handle unexpected spikes in traffic or usage.
6. To meet the performance and quality standards required by customers or regulatory bodies.

Q6 In what ways can Postman be utilized for testing and debugging APIs?

To use Postman to test and debug APIs, you can follow these steps:

1. Open Postman and create a new request.
2. Set the request method (GET, POST, PUT, DELETE, etc.) and the endpoint URL of the API you want to test.
3. Set the necessary headers and parameters for the API request.
4. Send the request and view the response in the "Response" tab of Postman.
5. Use the "Tests" feature of Postman to write test scripts to validate the response data and ensure that the API is functioning correctly.
6. Debug any issues with the API by examining the request and response data in Postman, and making adjustments as necessary.

Postman also provides features for organizing and managing your API requests, collaborating with team members, and automating your testing workflows.

Q7 Describe the benefits of Postman API?

There are several benefits of using Postman for API testing and development:

1. **Efficient testing:** Postman allows developers to efficiently test APIs by providing a user-friendly interface and a range of testing tools.
2. **Debugging:** With Postman, developers can easily debug their APIs by inspecting request and response payloads, headers, and status codes.
3. **Collaboration:** Postman makes it easy for teams to collaborate on API development and testing by allowing users to share collections, test results, and documentation.
4. **Automation:** Postman supports the automation of API testing and integration with popular CI/CD tools, making it easier to incorporate API testing into the development process.

5. **Documentation:** Postman allows developers to create detailed API documentation, making it easier for other developers to understand and use the API.

6. **Integration:** Postman integrates with a wide range of API development tools and services, including GitHub, Swagger, and AWS, among others.

Overall, Postman helps developers to save time and effort in API testing and development, resulting in faster time to market and improved software quality.

Q8 Provide a brief explanation of how Postman work?

Postman is an API development and testing tool that streamlines the development process by enabling developers to design, test, and document APIs in a single platform. The working mechanism of Postman is as follows:

1. **Designing APIs:** In Postman, developers can create APIs by defining requests, specifying headers and parameters, and creating mock responses.

2. **Testing APIs:** Postman allows developers to test APIs by sending requests, viewing and analyzing responses, and running automated tests to ensure proper functionality.

3. **Collaboration:** Postman provides collaboration features that allow team members to work on API development and testing together.

4. **Monitoring:** Postman also allows developers to monitor APIs in production, tracking performance and detecting issues.

5. **Documentation:** Postman automatically generates API documentation, making it easy for developers to share documentation with other team members or external users.

Overall, Postman simplifies the API development process by providing a comprehensive set of tools to design, test, and monitor APIs.

Q9 Explain what is meant by the "success type" status in Postman.

In Postman, the success status type refers to the HTTP status codes that indicate a successful response from the server. These are typically the 2xx series status codes such as 200 OK, 201 Created, 204 No Content, etc.

When a request in Postman returns a success status, it means that the request was successfully processed by the server and the desired response was returned without any errors. The success status type in Postman is represented by a green color and is accompanied by a checkmark icon.

Q10 Can you provide an explanation of Postman's testing mechanism?

Postman provides various testing mechanisms to validate the API response. The testing mechanism includes writing scripts to test the API response.

Postman has a built-in testing framework called "Postman Test Scripts," which allows the user to write tests in JavaScript. The test script is written in the "Tests" tab, which is available after making a request.

The following is an example of a test script in Postman:

```
// Tests if the response code is 200 OK
pm.test("Status code is 200", function () {
    pm.response.to.have.status(200);
});

// Tests if the response has a specific header
pm.test("Content-Type is present", function () {
    pm.response.to.have.header("Content-Type");
    pm.response.to.be.ok;
});
```

```
// Tests if the response has a specific JSON data
pm.test("Response body contains correct JSON data",
function () { var jsonData = pm.response.json();
    pm.expect(jsonData.name).to.eql("Testing");
});
```

In the above example, the script tests whether the response has a 200 OK status code, a specific header, and specific JSON data. If any of the tests fail, the test script will return an error message.

Postman also provides a feature called "Pre-request scripts," which allows the user to write scripts that are executed before making a request. These scripts are useful for setting variables or headers that are required for the request.

Overall, Postman's testing mechanism is robust and flexible, allowing the user to write custom scripts to validate the API response.

Q11 Can you provide an explanation of parameters in Postman?

In Postman, parameters refer to the dynamic values that are sent along with the API requests. These parameters can be defined in the URL, request body, headers, or any other part of the request.

Postman supports different types of parameters, such as:

1. **Query Parameters:** These parameters are included in the URL and are used to filter, sort, or search data.
2. **Path Parameters:** These parameters are used to identify a specific resource in the API path. They are included in the URL path and are enclosed in curly braces {}.
3. **Request Body Parameters:** These parameters are sent in the request body

and are used to pass additional data such as JSON or XML.

4. **Header Parameters:** These parameters are included in the request headers and are used to provide additional information about the request, such as authentication tokens, content type, etc.

In Postman, parameters can be easily added or modified using the Params tab. They can be set as static or dynamic values using variables, which can be stored and reused across requests.

Q12 Can you explain the various types of status codes in Postman?

In Postman, there are five main categories of status codes:

1. **Informational (100-199):** This category indicates that the request has been received and understood, but further action may be needed to fulfill the request.
2. **Success (200-299):** This category indicates that the request was successful and the server was able to fulfill the request as expected.
3. **Redirection (300-399):** This category indicates that the client must take additional action to complete the request. For example, the requested resource might have moved to a different location.
4. **Client Errors (400-499):** This category indicates that there was an error with the request, typically due to invalid or missing data. For example, a 404 Not Found error indicates that the requested resource could not be found.
5. **Server Errors (500-599):** This category indicates that there was an error on the server side while processing the request. For example, a 500 Internal Server Error indicates that the server encountered an unexpected condition that prevented it from fulfilling the request.

Q13 Explain the methodology for designing and developing APIs using Postman?

The following is a general methodology for API design and development in Postman:

1. **Identify the purpose of the API:** Determine the need for the API and what it is supposed to accomplish. Define the requirements and the expected results.
2. **Define the API endpoints:** Create a list of all the endpoints for the API. An endpoint is a specific URL that an API service responds to.
3. **Define the API parameters:** Determine the input and output parameters of each endpoint. Input parameters include any data that needs to be passed in a request to the endpoint. Output parameters include any data returned by the API.
4. **Design the API schema:** Create a schema or structure that defines the API. This includes the data formats used for input and output parameters, as well as any error-handling protocols.
5. **Test the API:** Use Postman to test the API to ensure that it is working properly. This includes checking for errors, verifying that input parameters are being properly processed, and confirming that the output parameters are returning the expected results.
6. **Document the API:** Create documentation for the API that explains how it works, how to use it, and how to troubleshoot any issues that may arise.
7. **Publish the API:** Publish the API so that it is available for use by other developers and applications. This includes registering the API with a service registry, setting up API security, and providing documentation and support for developers who will be using the API.

Q14 Can you provide examples of common uses for Postman?

Some typical uses of Postman include:

1. **Testing APIs:** Postman can be used to test APIs, including RESTful and SOAP APIs. You can send requests to the API, inspect the response, and debug issues.
2. **Automating API testing:** Postman can be used to automate API testing, allowing you to run a suite of tests automatically and receive feedback on the results.
3. **Documenting APIs:** Postman can be used to create API documentation, including descriptions of endpoints, request and response formats, and example requests and responses.
4. **Collaborating on APIs:** Postman can be used to share APIs with team members, allowing multiple people to work on the same API collection.
5. **Load testing APIs:** Postman can be used to perform load testing on APIs, allowing you to see how the API performs under heavy load.

Q15 How can a request be created in Postman?

To create a request in Postman, follow these steps:

1. Open Postman and click on the "New" button in the top-left corner.
2. Choose the type of request you want to create (GET, POST, PUT, DELETE, etc.) from the drop-down menu.
3. Enter the URL of the API endpoint you want to test in the "Enter request URL" field.
4. Select the appropriate HTTP method for the request.
5. Add any required request headers or parameters in the "Headers" and "Params" sections.
6. If necessary, add a request body in the "Body" section.
7. Click on the "Send" button to send the request to the API and view the

response.

Q16 Can you explain the configuration and usage of Postman environments?

Postman environments are configurations that enable a set of key-value pairs, which can be used across API requests. These key-value pairs may include URLs, authentication tokens, headers, or any other parameters that are required to make the API requests.

To configure a new environment, click on the 'gear' icon in the top-right corner of the Postman window, and select 'Manage Environments.' From here, you can add, edit, or delete an environment. Once an environment is created, it can be selected from the dropdown menu in the top-right corner of the Postman window. This allows users to quickly switch between different environments while sending API requests.

Q17 What is the mechanism behind saving and organizing requests in Postman?

In Postman, requests can be saved in different ways, including:

1. **Collections:** A collection is a group of related requests that can be organized together. Collections allow users to save and share their requests with others, as well as manage and organize them in a hierarchical structure.
2. **Environments:** An environment is a set of key-value pairs that define variables used in requests. For example, an environment can define the base URL for requests, or set authentication parameters. Environments allow users to create different sets of variables for different environments, such as development, staging, or production.
3. **Folders:** Folders are used to group requests within a collection. They provide an additional level of organization and help users to keep their

requests in a logical order.

4. **History:** Postman also maintains a history of requests that have been sent, which can be useful for reviewing past actions or repeating previous requests.

Q18 What are the methods for automating tasks using the Postman API?

The Postman API can be used to automate operations by integrating with other tools and scripts. This can be done by using the Postman API key to make authenticated requests to the Postman API endpoints.

Some of the operations that can be automated using the Postman API include:

1. **Collection Runs:** You can use the Postman API to trigger collection runs and get the results of the runs.
2. **Environment Management:** You can use the Postman API to create, update, and delete environments and environment variables.
3. **Script Execution:** You can use the Postman API to run scripts in a collection or a request.
4. **User Management:** You can use the Postman API to manage users, teams, and workspaces in Postman.

By using the Postman API to automate these operations, you can save time and effort in your testing and development workflows.

Q19 What are the troubleshooting methods for resolving issues encountered while using Postman?

When using Postman, problems can occur due to various reasons such as incorrect configuration, connectivity issues, or bugs in the software. To fix these problems, here are some steps that can be followed:

1. **Check the request configuration:** Ensure that the request is configured correctly with the right parameters, headers, and data.
2. **Check network connectivity:** Verify that the internet connection is stable and the API server is reachable.
3. **Update Postman:** Check if there are any updates available for Postman and install them to ensure the latest bug fixes and features are available.
4. **Clear cache and cookies:** Clearing the cache and cookies of the browser can help resolve some issues related to authentication and connectivity.
5. **Contact support:** If the problem persists, contact the Postman support team or community forums for assistance.

By following these steps, many of the common problems that occur while using Postman can be resolved.

Q20 What is the process of testing API endpoints with Postman?

To test API endpoints using Postman, we can follow these steps:

1. Open Postman and create a new request.
2. Select the HTTP method that the API endpoint supports (GET, POST, PUT, DELETE, etc.).
3. Enter the URL of the API endpoint.
4. Add any required headers or parameters.
5. Click the "Send" button to send the request.
6. Check the response to see if it is the expected response.

7. Repeat for other API endpoints that need to be tested.

Additionally, we can use Postman's built-in testing capabilities to automate the testing process and ensure that responses meet the expected criteria. This can be done using scripts that run after the request is sent and can check for specific values, headers, or other response attributes.

Q21 Can Postman be used to mock API endpoints?

Postman provides a feature called "Mock Servers" that allows you to simulate an API endpoint. To use this feature, you need to create a mock server in Postman and define the API response you want to simulate.

Here are the steps to create a mock server in Postman:

1. Open Postman and select the "Mocks" tab on the left-hand side.
2. Click on the "Create a Mock Server" button.
3. Choose the collection you want to create the mock server for.
4. Select the environment variables you want to use.
5. Choose a name for your mock server and click "Create Mock Server."
6. You will be redirected to a new page with the URL of your mock server.

Now, to mock an API endpoint using Postman:

1. Select the mock server you created from the "Mocks" tab.
2. Click on the "New Example" button.
3. Choose the method (GET, POST, etc.) and enter the endpoint URL.
4. Enter the expected response in the "Response" section.
5. Click "Save Example" and your API endpoint is now mocked.

You can now use the mocked API endpoint to test your client-side application.

Q22 Can Postman be used to describe APIs?

Postman provides a feature called "API documentation" that allows users to create comprehensive documentation for their APIs. To describe an API using Postman, you can follow these steps:

1. **Create a collection:** A collection is a group of requests that belong to a single API. Create a collection for the API that you want to describe.
2. **Create requests:** Create requests for each endpoint in the API. Add headers, parameters, and any other necessary information to each request.
3. **Add descriptions:** Add descriptions to each request, explaining what it does and what parameters it requires.
4. **Use markdown:** Postman supports markdown syntax, so you can use it to format your descriptions and make them more readable.
5. **Add examples:** Add examples to each request to show how it can be used.
6. **Publish the documentation:** Once you have created the documentation, you can publish it using Postman's built-in publishing feature. This will create a public URL that can be shared with others.

Q23 What is the process to send a PUT request using Postman?

To give a PUT request in Postman, follow these steps:

1. Open Postman and create a new request by clicking on the "New" button.
2. Select the "PUT" method from the dropdown menu next to the URL field.
3. Enter the endpoint URL in the URL field.
4. If necessary, add any required headers or parameters.
5. Enter the request body data in the "Body" tab. This can be in the form of raw data, a file, or form-data.
6. Click the "Send" button to submit the request.
7. View the response in the "Response" tab to verify that the request was

successful.

Note: PUT requests are typically used to update existing resources on the server, so make sure that you have the appropriate permissions to make changes to the resource.

Q24 What is the process to set a global variable in Postman?

To set a global variable in Postman, follow these steps:

1. Open the Postman application and click on the "Manage Environments" button located on the top-right corner of the window.
2. In the "Manage Environments" window, click on the "Globals" tab.
3. Click on the "Add" button to create a new global variable.
4. Enter the variable name in the "Key" field and the variable value in the "Initial Value" field.
5. Click on the "Save" button to save the global variable.

Once the global variable is created, it can be used in any request by enclosing the variable name inside double curly braces (e.g., **{{variable_name}}**).

Q25 Describe the process of creating a secure and scalable API management system for a large enterprise with multiple microservices?

Designing and implementing a secure and scalable API management system for a large enterprise with multiple microservices involves several steps:

1. **Identify the APIs:** The first step is to identify the APIs that need to be managed. This requires collaboration with various teams and stakeholders to understand the needs and requirements of each microservice.

2. **Standardize API design:** Once the APIs have been identified, it is important to standardize the design to ensure consistency across all the microservices. This includes defining the API specifications, including the request and response formats, HTTP methods, and parameters.

3. **Implement API gateway:** An API gateway acts as a single entry point for all the APIs and routes the requests to the appropriate microservice. It also provides security, authentication, rate limiting, and traffic management features.

4. **Ensure security:** Security is a critical aspect of API management. Implement security features such as authentication, authorization, and encryption to ensure that the APIs are protected from unauthorized access and misuse.

5. **Implement rate limiting and throttling:** Implementing rate limiting and throttling features helps in managing the traffic and ensures that the APIs are not overloaded.

6. **Monitor and analyze the APIs:** Use monitoring and analytics tools to track the performance and usage of the APIs. This helps in identifying and addressing issues before they become critical.

7. **Ensure scalability:** The API management system should be designed to handle a large volume of traffic and should be scalable to meet the growing needs of the enterprise.

Overall, designing and implementing a secure and scalable API management system requires a comprehensive understanding of the enterprise's needs, the microservices architecture, and the API design principles. It also requires collaboration between various teams and stakeholders, including developers, operations, security, and management.

Q26 Explain the process of integrating third-party tools and services with Postman?

Postman provides the ability to integrate with third-party tools, which helps to streamline the API testing and development process. Some examples of third-party integrations with Postman are:

1. **Newman:** Newman is a command-line collection runner for Postman. It can be integrated with Postman to run tests in CI/CD pipelines, generate reports, and execute collections programmatically.
2. **Jenkins:** Jenkins is an open-source automation server that can be used to automate the build, test, and deployment process. Postman can be integrated with Jenkins to run tests as part of a continuous integration pipeline.
3. **Swagger:** Swagger is a popular API documentation and design tool. Postman can be used to import Swagger files and generate API requests from the Swagger schema.
4. **Slack:** Slack is a popular team communication tool. Postman can be integrated with Slack to notify team members when a collection run has completed or when a test fails.
5. **GitHub:** GitHub is a code hosting platform that provides version control and collaboration features. Postman can be integrated with GitHub to manage collections, sync changes, and collaborate with team members.

To integrate third-party tools with Postman, users can leverage Postman's APIs and webhooks. For example, Newman can be used to execute Postman collections in a command-line interface, and the results can be reported back to Postman using webhooks. Similarly, Postman can be used to trigger Jenkins builds and generate reports based on the results.

Q27 Can you explain the steps involved in implementing a secure bearer token?

Bearer tokens are used to secure API endpoints by providing a unique access token to the user, which is validated with each API request. Here are the steps to implement a secure bearer token in Postman:

1. **Generate a unique token:** You can use a token generator or create one using any secure random string generator.
2. **Set up a token endpoint:** The token endpoint should accept authentication credentials and return a bearer token.
3. **Set up the token header:** In Postman, add an Authorization header with the bearer token value.
4. **Set up token validation:** The token should be validated with each API request to ensure it's still valid.
5. **Set up token expiration:** Bearer tokens should have a defined expiration time to ensure they are regularly updated and not abused.
6. **Set up token revocation:** In case of any security issues, it's important to have a way to revoke the bearer token.

By following these steps, you can implement a secure bearer token in Postman to protect your API endpoints.

Q28 How does Postman handle dynamic variables?

Dynamic variables in Postman can be managed using the built-in variables or by creating custom variables. The following steps can be followed to manage dynamic variables in Postman:

1. **Built-in variables:** Postman provides a set of built-in variables that

can be used to manage dynamic data. Some of the common built-in variables include **{{$guid}}**, **{{$timestamp}}**, **{{$randomInt}}**, **{{$randomString}}**, etc. These variables can be used to generate random data, timestamps, or unique identifiers.

2. **Environment variables:** Environment variables can be used to store data that needs to be shared across requests. To create an environment variable, go to the "Manage Environments" section in Postman and add a new environment. Then, add a variable by providing a key-value pair.

3. **Global variables:** Global variables can be used to store data that needs to be shared across different collections. To create a global variable, go to the "Globals" tab in Postman and add a new variable by providing a key-value pair.

4. **Custom variables:** Custom variables can be created using the "pm.variables.set()" method in the Postman scripting environment. This method can be used to set a value for a custom variable based on a specific condition or response from an API call.

By managing dynamic variables in Postman, testers can easily automate the testing process and reduce the effort required to test APIs with dynamic data.

Q29 What is the process to generate an authentication token using Postman?

To create an authentication token in Postman, follow these steps:

1. Open Postman and create a new request.
2. Select the "Authorization" tab.
3. Choose the type of authentication you want to use. This could be "Basic Auth", "OAuth 2.0", "API Key", or "Bearer Token".
4. Fill in the required authentication details, such as the username and password for Basic Auth or the access token for OAuth 2.0.
5. Click "Update Request" to save the authentication details.

Once you have created the authentication token, you can use it in your API requests by selecting the "Authorization" tab and choosing the appropriate type of authentication. The token will be automatically added to the request header when you send the request.

Q30 In Postman, how can I modify a request in a collection?

To modify a request in a collection in Postman, follow these steps:

1. Open the collection in Postman.
2. Click on the folder or sub-folder containing the request you want to modify.
3. Locate the request in the list of requests and click on it to open it.
4. Make the desired modifications to the request in the request builder.
5. Click the "Save" button to save the changes to the request.

Note: If the collection is synced with Postman cloud, the changes will be automatically updated in the cloud. If the collection is not synced, you will need to export the updated collection and share it with your team manually.

Q31 What would be your approach to designing a maintainable and scalable Postman collection for testing a RESTful API?

Designing a Postman collection for testing a RESTful API involves the following steps to ensure maintainability and scalability:

1. Identify the API endpoints and the expected responses.
2. Group the endpoints by functionality or resource.
3. Create a folder for each group and add the related endpoints to the folder.
4. Define variables for the API base URL, authentication credentials, and other dynamic values.
5. Use pre-request scripts and tests to handle dynamic values and automate repetitive tasks.
6. Use environment variables to manage configurations for different environments.
7. Define shared scripts and functions to avoid duplication of code.
8. Use Postman's built-in features like test suites, data-driven testing, and test reports to automate testing and ensure consistent results.
9. Use version control to manage changes to the collection and collaborate with team members.
10. Continuously refine the collection by adding new endpoints, updating tests, and improving documentation.

By following these steps, the Postman collection can be well-organized, modular, and maintainable, making it easier to manage and scale testing efforts for a RESTful API.

Q32 What are the steps to share a Postman collection?

To share a collection in Postman, follow these steps:

1. Open the collection you want to share.

2. Click on the "Share" button located in the top right corner of the Postman window.

3. In the pop-up window, choose the sharing option that best suits your needs. You can choose to share the collection via a link, email, or with a Postman team.

4. If you choose to share via a link, you can set access permissions and add an expiration date for the link.

5. Click "Share" to complete the sharing process.

Once you have shared the collection, other users can import it into their own Postman application and use it to test the RESTful API.

Q33 What is the process to import a collection from a link in Postman?

To import a collection from a link in Postman, follow these steps:

1. Open Postman and click on the "Import" button located on the top-left corner of the app window.

2. Select the "Link" tab.

3. Enter the URL or link of the collection that you want to import in the "Link" field.

4. If the collection is public, you can directly click on the "Import" button. If the collection is private, you need to enter the credentials to authenticate the request.

5. Once you click on the "Import" button, Postman will start importing the collection from the provided link.

After importing, you can find the collection in the "Collections" tab of Postman

Q34 What are the steps to import a collection from a code snippet in Postman?

To import a collection from a code snippet in Postman, follow these steps:

1. Open Postman and click on the "Import" button located on the top-left corner of the window.
2. In the "Import" modal, select the "Code" tab.
3. Select the programming language of your choice and copy the code snippet that contains the collection.
4. Paste the code snippet in the "Paste Code" section of the modal.
5. Click on the "Import" button to import the collection.

Once the collection is imported, you can view it in the left-hand sidebar under the "Collections" tab.

Q35 What is the process to view network logs in Postman?

To view network logs in Postman, you can follow these steps:

1. Open Postman and make a request to the API endpoint that you want to view the network logs.
2. Click on the "Console" button in the bottom left corner of the Postman window.
3. In the console window that appears, click on the "Network" tab to view the network logs for your request.
4. You can filter the logs by selecting the "All," "XHR," or "WS" tabs at the top of the network logs section.
5. You can also filter the logs by searching for specific terms using the search bar at the top of the console window.

By following these steps, you can view and analyze the network logs for your requests in Postman.

Q36 In Postman, how can I create a custom timeout for a request?

To set a custom timeout for a request in Postman, follow these steps:

1. Open the request you want to set a timeout for.
2. Click on the "Settings" icon in the top-right corner of the request panel.
3. In the "Request" tab of the settings, scroll down to the "Timeout" section.
4. Check the "Override timeout" checkbox to enable the custom timeout setting.
5. Enter the desired timeout value in milliseconds in the "Timeout (ms)" field.
6. Save the changes by clicking the "Save" button.

After setting the custom timeout, Postman will wait for the specified time before timing out the request. This can be useful for testing APIs with slow response times or when dealing with network issues.

Q37 In Postman, how can I activate or disable automatic follow redirects?

To enable or disable automatic follow redirects in Postman, follow these steps:

1. Open the request in Postman for which you want to enable or disable automatic follow redirects.
2. Click on the "Settings" button located on the right side of the request URL input box.
3. In the "Settings" menu, scroll down to the "Follow Redirects" option.
4. To enable automatic follow redirects, turn on the toggle switch next to "Follow Redirects". To disable it, turn it off.

5. Once done, click on the "Save" button to save the changes.

By enabling automatic follow redirects, Postman will automatically follow any redirects returned by the server, while disabling it will not allow Postman to automatically follow any redirects.

Q38 Explain the different terminologies related to HTTP authentication and their applications in Postman?

HTTP authentication is a mechanism for providing access control to web resources. There are several types of HTTP authentication used in Postman:

1. **Basic Authentication:** It is the simplest authentication mechanism used for authentication with a username and password.
2. **Digest Authentication:** This authentication type uses a message digest to provide a more secure authentication mechanism than basic authentication.
3. **OAuth 1.0a:** It is an authentication protocol used for securing API requests. It requires an access token, access token secret, consumer key, and consumer secret.
4. **OAuth 2.0:** This authentication type is an extension of OAuth 1.0a, providing authorization for users to access web resources using access tokens.
5. **API Key Authentication:** It is a type of authentication that uses an API key to authenticate users and provide access to the resources.

In Postman, these authentication types can be added to a request in the Authorization tab of the request builder.

Q39 Explain postman cloud?

Postman Cloud is a cloud-based collaboration platform for API development. It allows developers to share and collaborate on Postman collections, workspaces, and environments. With Postman Cloud, team members can work together on API development projects, track changes, and share feedback in real-time. It also provides features like version control, team management, and usage analytics.

Q40 Can you explain how to create and use Postman collections?

To create and use a Postman collection, follow these steps:

1. Open Postman and create a new collection by clicking on the "New" button in the top-left corner of the interface.
2. Give your collection a name and description.
3. Add requests to your collection by clicking on the "Add Request" button and filling out the necessary information, such as the URL and HTTP method.
4. Organize your requests within the collection by creating folders and subfolders.
5. Save your collection by clicking on the "Save" button in the top-right corner of the interface.
6. To use your collection, simply click on the name of the collection in the left-hand sidebar and select the request you want to send.

Q41 How can I access the Postman console?

The Postman console is used to view logs and debug requests in real-time. It can be accessed from the Postman app by clicking on the "Console" button at the bottom of the window. The console displays information about requests and responses, including headers, status codes, and timings. It can also be used to send test requests and view the corresponding responses. The console is a useful tool for troubleshooting issues in API testing and development.

Q42 How to make use of Postman scripts?

In Postman, scripts can be used to automate certain tasks and to perform customizations. To use Postman scripts, follow these steps:

1. Open the Postman app and create a new request or open an existing one.
2. Click on the "Tests" tab.
3. Write the script in the text editor provided. Scripts can be written in JavaScript.
4. Save the script by clicking the "Save" button.
5. Run the script by clicking the "Send" button. The script will execute automatically after the response is received.

Postman scripts can be used to automate tasks such as setting environment variables, parsing and validating responses, and extracting data from responses to be used in subsequent requests.

Q43 What are the steps to configure the Postman environment to store variables that can be utilized across multiple requests?

To set up the Postman environment to store variables that can be used for multiple requests, you can follow these steps:

1. Click on the "Manage Environments" button in the top right corner of the Postman window.
2. Click on the "Add" button to create a new environment.
3. Give the environment a name and add any variables that you want to store for this environment.
4. Once the environment is created, select it from the dropdown menu in the top right corner of the Postman window.
5. Use the syntax **{{variable_name}}** in your requests to reference the stored variables.

For example, if you have a variable called **base_url** in your environment, you can use it in your request URL like this: **{{base_url}}/api/users**.

By storing variables in environments, you can easily switch between different sets of variables for different environments (e.g. development, staging, production) and keep your requests consistent across multiple requests.

Q44 How can I ensure that the response has specific data?

To test the response in Postman and make sure it contains specific data, you can use tests and assertions. Here are the steps to do this:

1. Send a request to the API endpoint.
2. Click on the "Tests" tab in the Postman request editor.
3. Write a test script in JavaScript that extracts the required data from the response and checks whether it is present or not.
4. Use the Postman assertion library to write assertions that verify the expected behavior of the API.
5. Save the test script and run the test.

For example, if you want to test whether the response body contains a specific string, you can write the following test script:

```
pm.test("Response contains specific string", function () {
    var jsonData = pm.response.json();
    pm.expect(jsonData.name).to.include("specific string");
});
```

This script extracts the "name" attribute from the response JSON and checks whether it includes the "specific string" or not. If the string is present, the test passes, otherwise, it fails.

Q45 Explain OAuth?

OAuth is an authorization framework that allows users to grant access to their resources stored in one service to a third-party application without sharing their credentials. It works by having the user authorize the third-party application to access their resources, after which the application receives an access token that can be used to access those resources.

Q46 Can I configure a Postman collection to execute a set of requests in a specific order?

To configure a Postman collection to execute a set of requests in a specific order, you can use the "Runner" feature of Postman. Here are the steps:

1. Open your collection in Postman.
2. Click on the "Runner" button located at the top-right corner of the app.
3. In the "Runner" window, select your collection from the drop-down menu.
4. Select the environment you want to use (if you have set up one).
5. Under the "Collection Run" tab, select the order in which you want to execute your requests.
6. Click on the "Start Run" button.

You can also use the "Pre-request Script" feature in each request to set up dependencies between requests. This way, you can ensure that a certain request is executed only after another request has completed successfully.

Q47 How can I insert dynamic variables into the request URL?

In Postman, you can use dynamic variables in the request URL by enclosing the variable name within curly braces {}. Here are the steps to use dynamic variables in the request URL:

1. **Set up the variables:** You can set up variables by defining them in the environment or collection, or by using scripts to generate them dynamically.
2. **Use the variable in the URL:** In the request URL, replace the fixed value with the variable name enclosed in curly braces. For example, if you have a variable named id, you can use it in the URL as https://example.com/api/{id}.

3. **Select the variable in the Params tab:** In the Params tab, select the variable from the dropdown list to add it to the URL.

4. **Set the variable value:** Set the value of the variable in the environment or collection or using pre-request scripts.

Q48 How can I integrate Slack into Postman?

Integrating Slack with Postman allows you to receive notifications for various events in your Postman workflows. Here are the steps to integrate Slack with Postman:

1. Open your Postman account and navigate to the Integrations tab.
2. Click on the Slack app and click on the Install button.
3. Enter your Slack workspace URL and click on the Install button.
4. Follow the prompts to authorize Postman to access your Slack workspace.
5. Once authorized, you can configure the Slack integration settings, such as which events to trigger notifications for and where to send them.
6. Save the settings and start using the integration.

You can also use Slack with Postman through the use of webhooks, which allow you to send data from Postman to a Slack channel or user. To use webhooks, you will need to create a webhook in Slack and then configure Postman to send data to that webhook.

Q49 In Jenkins, how do I configure Postman environments and variables?

Setting up Postman environments and variables in Jenkins involves the following steps:

1. Install the Postman plugin in Jenkins.
2. Create a new Jenkins job and configure it to use the Postman plugin.
3. In the job configuration, specify the Postman collection file and environ-

ment file.

4. Add build steps to the job to execute the Postman collection using the Postman plugin.

5. Set up the environment variables in the Jenkins job to store the values needed for the Postman collection and environment files.

6. Use the Jenkins environment variables in the Postman environment file to configure dynamic values.

7. Run the Jenkins job to execute the Postman collection with the specified environment variables.

Overall, this integration allows for automated testing of APIs using Postman collections within the Jenkins continuous integration and deployment pipeline.

Q50 What is the process of using Postman to send requests to multiple servers or environments?

To send requests to multiple environments or servers using Postman, you can use Postman's built-in functionality to manage environments.

1. Open Postman and click on the "Manage Environments" button in the top right corner of the window.

2. Click on "Add" to create a new environment and give it a name. You can define variables for this environment by adding a key and value.

3. Repeat the above step to create environments for each server you want to send requests to.

4. Create a new collection by clicking on the "New" button in the top left corner of the window.

5. Add the requests you want to send to each environment to the collection.

6. For each request, click on the "Environment Quick Look" button on the top right of the request editor, and select the environment you want to send the request to.

7. Repeat the above step for all requests in the collection.

8. Click on the "Runner" button in the top right corner of the window to open the Runner.

9. Select the collection you want to run from the list, and select the environments you want to run the collection against.

10. Click "Run" to send the requests to the specified environments/servers.

Q51 What are the steps to integrate Postman with continuous integration platforms such as Jenkins to run API tests automatically as a part of a build process?

Postman can be integrated with continuous integration (CI) platforms like Jenkins using the Postman API. Here are the steps to integrate Postman with Jenkins:

1. **Install the Postman Jenkins plugin:** Install the Postman Jenkins plugin from the Jenkins plugin manager. This plugin allows you to run your Postman collections as part of your Jenkins build process.

2. **Generate a Postman API key:** Generate an API key from the Postman dashboard. This API key is used to authenticate the Postman plugin in Jenkins.

3. **Configure the Postman plugin in Jenkins:** In the Jenkins global configuration, enter the Postman API key and configure other settings such as the collection file path and environment file path.

4. **Add Postman build step to your Jenkins job:** In your Jenkins job configuration, add a Postman build step and specify the collection, environment, and other settings.

5. **Run your Jenkins job:** Run your Jenkins job to execute your Postman collection.

With this integration, Jenkins will automatically run your Postman collection as part of your build process and report any test failures or errors.

Q52 What are the methods to simulate various network conditions, such as low bandwidth or high latency, using Postman for API performance testing?

Postman provides a built-in feature called "Interceptor" that can be used to simulate different network conditions. Interceptor allows users to capture API requests made through an external system like a browser, and then replay them in Postman with various network conditions applied.

To simulate high latency or low bandwidth, users can apply network throttling to the captured requests using Interceptor. This can be done by selecting the "Network" tab in Interceptor, and then choosing the desired network conditions from the drop-down menu. Users can also set custom network conditions by specifying the desired latency and bandwidth values.

Additionally, Postman provides a feature called "Collection Runner" that can be used to run collections of API requests with various network conditions applied. Users can configure the network conditions for each request in the collection using the same methods as described above, and then run the collection to see how the API performs under adverse conditions. This can help identify any performance issues or bottlenecks in the API, allowing for optimization and improvement.

Q53 What are the steps to debug in Postman?

Debugging in Postman involves troubleshooting and identifying issues in requests and responses. Here are the steps to debug in Postman:

1. Check the request URL and make sure it is correct.
2. Ensure the request headers and parameters are set up correctly.
3. Use the Postman console to view the request and response logs.
4. Check the response status code and body to identify any errors or issues.

5. Use the Postman console to view the network logs and identify any issues with the request or response.
6. Use Postman scripts to add custom logic to requests and responses for debugging purposes.
7. Use the Postman Sandbox to execute JavaScript code for debugging.

By following these steps, you can effectively debug requests and responses in Postman and identify and resolve any issues or errors.

Q54 What are the steps to diagnose the root cause of a "500 Internal Server Error" response in an API when the error message is insufficient using Postman?

When you receive a "500 Internal Server Error" response from an API, it indicates that there is an issue on the server side. The error message returned by the server may not always provide enough information to identify the root cause of the problem. Here are some steps you can take to debug the issue using Postman:

1. **Check the request:** Ensure that the request you are sending is valid and contains all the required parameters.
2. **Check the response headers:** Check the response headers to see if they contain any useful information, such as a detailed error message or an error code.
3. **Use Postman Console:** Postman Console logs every request and response sent through Postman. You can use this to see if any errors or warnings are being generated by the API.
4. **Use Postman Interceptor:** Postman Interceptor allows you to capture HTTP traffic from your browser or system and import it into Postman. You can use this to capture the traffic when you reproduce the issue on your browser, and then analyze it in Postman to determine the root cause of the problem.

5. **Check the server logs:** Check the server logs to see if they contain any useful information about the error.

6. **Contact the server team:** If you are unable to determine the root cause of the problem using the above steps, you may need to contact the server team and provide them with the information you have gathered so far. They should be able to assist you in resolving the issue.

Q55 What are the steps to send an HTTP request for file upload functions using Postman?

To send an HTTP request using Postman for file upload functions, you can follow these steps:

1. Open Postman and create a new request.
2. Set the request type to "POST" and enter the endpoint URL.
3. Select the "Body" tab and choose the "form-data" option.
4. Add a new field for the file upload by clicking on the "Add More Fields" button.
5. Give the field a name, and select the "File" option from the dropdown.
6. Click on the "Choose Files" button and select the file you want to upload.
7. Add any additional form fields required by your API.
8. Click on the "Send" button to submit the request.
9. Check the response to verify that the file was uploaded successfully.

Note: Make sure that the endpoint supports file uploads and accepts the file in the format specified by the API.

Q56 How postman can be integrated with GraphQL

To integrate GraphQL and Postman, follow these steps:

1. Open Postman and create a new request.
2. In the request URL field, enter the URL of the GraphQL endpoint you want

to query.

3. In the request body tab, select GraphQL as the request type.

4. Enter your GraphQL query in the request body field.

5. In the request header tab, add a header with the key "Content-Type" and the value "application/json".

6. Send the request and review the response.

Note that GraphQL requests can be more complex than typical REST API requests, and may require more advanced knowledge of GraphQL syntax. Additionally, some GraphQL APIs may require authentication or authorization tokens to be included in the request headers.

Q57 How can I use Postman to test and debug a REST API?

To test and debug a REST API with Postman, follow these steps:

1. Import your API endpoints into a Postman collection. You can do this by manually creating requests, importing a Swagger or OpenAPI specification, or importing a JSON or CSV file containing request data.

2. Configure any required authorization settings for your API. This may include setting up OAuth or API keys.

3. Execute each request in your collection to ensure that the API is functioning as expected. You can use Postman's built-in test scripts to automatically validate the response data.

4. Use Postman's debugging tools to troubleshoot any issues that you encounter during testing. These tools may include the Console, Network Inspector, and the ability to view response headers and status codes.

5. Continuously iterate on your collection as you identify and resolve issues. You can use Postman's version control and collaboration features to manage changes and work with your team.

By following these steps, you can effectively test and debug your REST API using Postman, ensuring that it is working as intended before deploying it to production.

Also by Shubham Mishra

Web Penetration Testing: Hack Your Way

Nothing is more important than preserving security on websites. Internet security is a constantly evolving arena, forced to improve on a daily basis as malicious attempts become more sophisticated. The sad fact is many websites lack the necessary security to protect users or owners. This should not be the case. Web Penetration Testing is a beginner's guide focusing on WordPress penetration testing. Considering how popular WordPress has become it is an attractive target for hackers. Web Penetration Testing delivers important tools every website operator needs. Filled with useful information from newbie-pleasant interface to open-source tools, this book provides the first step to ensuring your site is secure from hackers. WordPress remains one of the most popular CRM sites, making it a constant target. Can you afford to be hacked? Web Penetration Testing delivers a robust and achievable system designed to help you stop, fix, and identify hacking attempts before they steal priceless information. The internet age is the greatest advancement the world has seen to date and your security on it vital.

Cyber Security Interview Q & A

Our lives forever changed in the late 1990s with the launch of the internet. A new age of technology was ushered in, complete with joys, challenges, and dangers. As advancements continue we are faced with a new danger that was once relegated to con men and grifters. Today we must contend with hackers gaining our critical information at unprecedented levels. Never before has protecting your personal data been so important, nor has the need for qualified cyber security experts.

Cyber Security Interview Questions & Answers is a comprehensive guide to understanding the field of cyber security and how to find the right fit for anyone seeking a job. From the mind of one of the world's leading cyber security experts, this book explores the various jobs in the field, such as:

Security software developer

Ethical hacker

Chief information security officer

Digital forensics expert

And more.

Cyber security is the fastest-growing industry on the planet. It is in a constant state of development as we race to keep up with new technologies. If you are ready to begin your next career, or just collecting information to make a decision, Cyber Security Interview Questions & Answers is the book for you.